T H E
BIG
DIVIDE

The Big

A Travel Guide to Historic & Civil War Sites

Divide

in the Missouri-Kansas Border Region

Diane Eickhoff & Aaron Barnhart

Quindaro Press • Kansas City

For our grandchildren

Sofia, Alex, Nico, and Malcolm

The Big Divide: A Travel Guide to Historic and Civil War Sites in the Missouri-Kansas Border Region

Quindaro Press
3808 Genessee Street
Kansas City, Missouri 64111
quindaropress.com
TheBigDivide.com

Library of Congress Control Number: 2013900125

ISBN-13 (paper): 978-0-9764434-1-4

All design (including cover design), graphics, and photography by Aaron Barnhart unless noted otherwise. Photos used with attribution from Wikimedia Commons are credited to their authors in the format username/wm.

Photo, title page: Konza Prairie near Manhattan, Kansas (Jared May/JaredKS.com)

Publisher's statement: Quindaro Press is grateful to the contributors of Wikimedia Commons for providing many of the images used in this work. The publisher has independently verified the public domain status of certain images used in this book, obtained permission to use others, and determined that the remainder are transformed by their use in this book, which constitutes fair use under the Copyright Act of 1976. See, for example, Aufderheide, Patricia and Peter Jaszi, *Reclaiming Fair Use: How to Put Balance Back in Copyright* (Chicago: University of Chicago Press, 2011), pages 127–147.

Got kids?

See "Ideas for Parents and Teachers" on page 224

Driving tours?

They're on page 122

Table of Contents

The Big Divide is also an e-book!

We know that many road-trippers enjoy the convenience of taking a mobile device for reading on the go. For those readers we offer *The Big Divide* in the most popular e-book formats, compatible with Kindle, Apple, Nook, and other e-readers. The e-book version is interactive, with links to websites mentioned in the print version, plus full-color photographs formatted for your mobile device.

The Big Divide is available at your favorite e-book store or by visiting our website — **TheBigDivide.com**.

How to Use This Guide

We wrote this book to share with you the remarkable story of the Missouri-Kansas border region as it is told through more than 130 historic sites, monuments, museums, parks, cemeteries, and shrines. That is the sole focus of *The Big Divide*. If you were looking for a list of area "attractions," restaurants or lodging recommendations, there are other guides that serve that purpose.

If, however, you are thinking about a road trip or day trip to explore the rich history of this region and want to make the most of your time, then you have come to the right place. *The Big Divide* offers multiple paths for exploring this vast region where some of the most consequential episodes in U.S. history took place.

We visited every site in this book, often more than once. Not every site is for every reader. Taken together, though, these sites tell a big story. If you have time to visit them all, like we did, you won't be sorry.

Take a few minutes to get familiar with the sections of *The Big Divide*, and soon you'll be planning your next great road trip.

- ☛ **Chapter maps:** These show the location of all sites in the chapter. The map numbers are included with the site listings for easy reference.

- ☛ **Driving tours:** If you're looking for themed driving tour ideas, we have eight of them, beginning on page 122. Most are thematic — African-American heritage, historic homes, etc. — and can be covered in a day or two.

- ☛ **Where am I?:** You can customize your driving tour easily by locating a site of interest, then using the Orientation Map on page 248 and the Index to find other interesting places nearby.

- ☛ **A Line in the Dirt:** Why we wrote *The Big Divide*.

- ☛ **Tips for the Trip:** Getting the most out of history travel.

- ☛ **Chapters:** Most travel guides are organized around geography. The chapters of *The Big Divide* are organized historically, starting with the time before civilization ("The Land") and continuing all the way through the 21st century ("Liberty and Justice").

- **Introductions:** Each chapter's introduction will help you understand how the sites in that chapter fit into the big picture — whether that is the history of westward migration, the border battles between Bushwhackers and Jayhawkers, or the quest for equal rights.

- **Site listing:** Each listing has the same basic information: site description, address, admission fees, accessibility, and contact information, followed by …

Our Take
A summary of our review.

… followed by the review.

- **Big Divide Top Sites:** We selected 16 of the sites in this book as the ones to visit if you only have time to make a few essential stops. You will see the "Big Divide Top Site" designation in its listing. We have also created a Top Sites Driving Tour (page 125).

- **"Near here" and cross-references:** We spent a lot of time thinking about how the sites relate to each other, both thematically and geographically. As a result, there are more than 100 cross-references in this book to help you explore related sites and make the unexpected discoveries that make history travel so much fun.

- **Spotlight:** At the end of chapters we shine a light on community museums of interest.

- **Extras:** Need to find the nearest visitor center? Want an enriching experience for your kids? How about some extra reading for the car, or some video to prepare for your trip? We have all this, plus a 200-year timeline and comprehensive index in the back.

Finally, we invite you to visit TheBigDivide.com and sign up for our mailing list — we'll send you a free gift just for joining. We also welcome your feedback for the next edition.

Now get ready to **take a ride on *The Big Divide.***

A Line in the Dirt

Outsiders may be forgiven for thinking that a river divides Missouri and Kansas. That is only true north of downtown Kansas City, Missouri. South of there the border runs invisibly for 150 miles, straight as an arrow to Arkansas. As you go back and forth across this unseen state line — driving the well-maintained roads from Olathe to Independence, Nevada to Fort Scott, Baxter Springs to Joplin — you may scarcely realize you are blithely tripping over one of the most turbulent and meaningful borders in the whole U. S. A.

This line in the dirt, at 94°61′ longitude, was created as a "permanent Indian boundary" when Missouri attained statehood in 1821. It was meant to separate white settlers from the Indian tribes who had been relentlessly pushed westward since colonial times. Later that border would be the contested line over the expansion of slavery. With nothing standing between them, Missourians and Kansans freely harassed each other during the Border War mayhem. Afterward, when the country became engulfed in Civil War, not only did the cross-border violence intensify but the divided loyalties among Missourians led to even more cruelty.

Being relative newcomers to the Missouri-Kansas border region, we can't help but notice how often people here identify with their side of the state line. The political space between them has narrowed to almost nothing; both states, for example, now reliably vote Republican in presidential elections. Despite this, folks let you know they are Missourians or they are Kansans, one or the other.

In our experience, though, most people know little about the history that supposedly divides them. They have some awareness of the exploits of John Brown and William Clarke Quantrill. Kansans know their state was on the right side of the slavery question and that Missouri was not. Missourians know that the University of Kansas Jayhawks are named for a band of notorious border raiders who ruthlessly plundered and burned Missouri farms and towns. Despite their sometimes sketchy recall, however, the people who live here take obvious pride in their history.

Of course, the deep schism between these two states — the big *divide* — has faded since the Civil War, reduced mostly to an athletic rivalry. Yet whether they know it or not, the people living along the Missouri-Kansas border today are inheritors to a vast trove of historic and cultural treasures that makes it a *big* divide — deep, expansive, and very interesting.

We want to take you to the places where that history and culture come alive in ways that no textbook or cable TV show can. For the cost of a tank of gas and a few admission fees, anyone can relive some of the most dramatic episodes in U.S. history and gain a better understanding of the heroes, villains, and forces that made this region, and in turn our country, what it is today.

Maybe we were always meant to write this book. Our friendship, and later marriage, was sparked more than 20 years ago watching the Ken Burns film *The Civil War* together at Diane's house. Aaron didn't own a TV set at the time, though eventually he got one, watched it quite a bit, and was hired by the *Kansas City Star* as its television critic.

We settled here in 1997, in an old house in a historic part of town, just two blocks east of the state line in Missouri, and soon we were taking weekend drives exploring the area. It was during a visit to the Wyandotte County Museum (page 36) that Diane was introduced to a 19th-century reformer and women's rights activist named Clarina Nichols, who had lived in Kansas during its most turbulent years. Meeting Nichols was the beginning of the end of

Diane's career as a textbook editor and the start of a new career in history. She became a speaker for the Kansas Humanities Council and we published her first biography, *Revolutionary Heart: The Life of Clarina Nichols and the Pioneering Crusade for Women's Rights,* in 2006.

Over time we came to learn much about the disparate histories of Kansas and Missouri. In 2010 we attended a presentation by the people who had helped create Freedom's Frontier, a new federally designated National Heritage Area. A grassroots effort years in the making, Freedom's Frontier will help promote cultural understanding and tourism in the Missouri-Kansas border region. The presentation convinced us that it was time to share our love of this region and its unique history with our readers. (For the record, *The Big Divide* is not a guide to Freedom's Frontier, and we have included a number of sites that are not part of Freedom's Frontier National Heritage Area.)

We decided to tell the region's story through its historic and cultural sites exclusively. While our story was about the border region, we gave ourselves permission to include any sites that were relevant to that story. That meant going as far west as Fort Riley, Kansas (page 42), and as far east as Arrow Rock, Missouri (page 152). It meant including not just large-scale sites with professional staff, like Wilson's Creek National Battlefield (page 111), but local museums with one-of-a-kind artifacts and distinctive stories to tell.

Diane had the idea to structure our book as a narrative, so that a person who read only the chapter introductions would get a complete history of the border region. Aaron, always the critic, took the lead on the site reviews.

We logged 4,000 miles in researching *The Big Divide,* and we have rarely had more fun together. We behaved like regular visitors — albeit ones who took notes and asked lots of questions (though we usually ask lots of questions anyway!). Sometimes we had our grandchildren in tow. In short, we wanted to experience these sites just as our readers and their families could expect to.

We want to thank Judy Billings, Fred Conboy, Julie McPike, Sonia Smith, and the site coordinators and partners who met for years and hashed out the details of Freedom's Frontier National Heritage Area. We could not have done this guide without their hard work.

We also want to acknowledge four historians who vetted portions of this book and made invaluable comments: Jeremy Neely, Jennifer Weber, Diane Mutti Burke, and Joan Stack. Carol Powers and Mary Lou Nolan made suggestions that greatly improved the look and utility of the guide. Of course, responsibility for any lingering errors herein rests with the coauthors.

Tips for the Trip

☞ **When to visit:** Spring and fall are long and glorious seasons in the lower Midwest. Summer heat can limit your time in parks and battlefields, though all the interiors are air-conditioned. Many sites have limited hours in winter. Check the websites of the places you want to visit ahead of time for upcoming programs and events — these are the best times to visit.

☞ **How much time:** Figure on one hour to visit each site — more time if you like reading all the signs. Large battlefields and major museums can take half a day or longer. If you're enjoying a site, don't be shy about asking for a re-entry ticket. Take a break to recover from the effects of "museumitis," then go back for more.

☞ **Before you visit:** *Call ahead or check the website.* Historic and cultural sites are not theme parks. Your experience will vary based on when you go and who is there to receive you. Smaller sites are run by volunteers. They can — and do — change their hours of operation. Call ahead to make sure someone's there who can show you around and answer questions. At press time National Park Service sites like the Noland Home (page 207) had been closed indefinitely due to staff shortages caused by mandated federal spending cuts.

☞ **Accessibility needs:** Wheelchair accessible sites are noted in our guide with the ♿ symbol. The staff at these sites often go out of their way to accommodate guests with special needs. *Call ahead.*

☞ **When you arrive:** Sign the guest book. It's proof of your visit; to a nonprofit organization that's like money in the bank. Next, watch the orientation film if one is playing. It will help you understand the site and the perspective of the people who built it. If there is a guided tour, take it. Cell phone tours are also good. Brochure or "self-guided" tours are better than nothing.

☞ **Interpretation:** You will see this word often in our guide. It simply means that someone has gone to the trouble of explaining the significance of the place where you are standing or the artifact you are looking at. It should not be confused with opinions ("well, that's *your* interpretation"). Well-interpreted sites are usually curated by professionals who know how to connect a roomful of objects into a coherent, compelling whole while understanding that historical events can be seen from various points of view. Other approaches, like handmade signs or a knowledgeable tour guide, can also provide good interpretation.

☞ **Get more out of your visit:** If you are visiting one of the county or community museums, be sure to ask your volunteer guide what ties to they have to the history on display. You'll be surprised at the responses! Pictures are great souvenirs, and we have found that most sites are happy to have you take them. But ask first, and don't forget to ID your pictures before you forget where you took them.

☞ **The gift shop by the exit:** Museum gift shops often carry unique items you won't find any place else. By buying their merchandise, you're helping keep the lights on. Keep friends and family in mind when visiting these sites.

☞ **Eat local:** We encourage you to skip the chains and delve into the homegrown diners and drive-ins of this region. When we travel, we prefer an old-school approach. Instead of the interstates, we take the "blue highways" and state roads, and we pack a lunch to eat at a roadside picnic table. (See "picnic-friendly sites" in the Index for recommendations.) If we're still hungry, we look for a pie shop in town.

☞ **How much you'll spend:** Most of the sites in this book are free. Unbelievable, right? In fact, an adult who visits all 130-plus sites in *The Big Divide* will pay admission fees totalling about $200. Seniors will pay less, and kids even less than that. Time rather than cost is the most important consideration when planning and taking your border road trip. Happy trails!

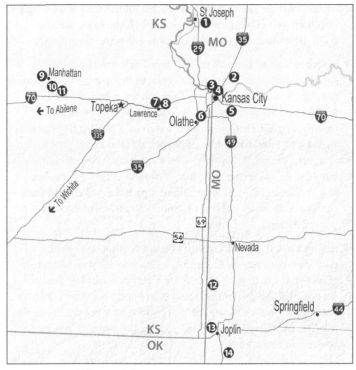

Sites in This Chapter

1. Remington Nature Center, St. Joseph, MO

2. Martha LaFite Thompson Nature Sanctuary, Liberty, MO

3. Anita B. Gorman Discovery Center, Kansas City, MO

4. Lakeside Nature Center, Kansas City, MO

5. Burr Oak Woods Nature Center, Blue Springs, MO

6. Ernie Miller Nature Center, Olathe, KS

7. KU Natural History Museum, Lawrence, KS

8. Prairie Park Nature Center, Lawrence, KS

9. Flint Hills Discovery Center, Manhattan, KS

10. Beecher Bible and Rifle Church, Wamego, KS

11. Mount Mitchell Heritage Prairie, Wamego, KS

12. Prairie State Park, Mindenmines, MO

13. Wildcat Glades, Joplin, MO

14. Neosho National Fish Hatchery, Neosho, MO

Tip: The Orientation Map on page 248 shows all Big Divide towns.

Mount Mitchell Heritage Prairie.

❧ 1 ❧

The Land

The Missouri-Kansas border region comprises some 20 million acres of fields, woodlands, river valleys, settlements, and cities. No journey into The Big Divide is complete without exploring the area's distinctive geography, for the land itself has helped shape the region's history.

In prehistoric times, what we now call the Midwestern United States lay submerged under a shallow sea that spanned the length of this continent. About 200 million years ago the water vanished, and the ocean floor — made of limestone and a tough-as-nails substrate called chert — became the prairie, a waving sea of tallgrass and wildflowers that was unrivaled for biological diversity and hypnotic beauty.

More than 95 percent of that prairie is now farmland or forest. What remains is mostly here, in the Flint Hills region of eastern Kansas, its rich grasses grazed upon by livestock, its splendor gazed upon by both artists and tourists. The Flint Hills are a source of state pride, as you will discover at the brand-new **Flint Hills Discovery Center** (page 16) in Manhattan, Kansas. A few miles down the road are the historically significant **Mount Mitchell Heritage Prairie** (page 10) and **Beecher Bible and Rifle Church** (page 12). Missouri is also preserving its tallgrass where it can, including **Prairie State Park** (page 9) just east of the state line.

Nature museums and centers are another place to learn about the region's geology, botany, and wildlife. **The University of Kansas Natural History Museum** (page 12) is the area's premier place to learn about the diversity of life forms that have lived off this land. A number of area **nature centers** (pages 13, 16, and 18–21) combine kid-friendly features like miniature zoos with hiking trails through restored tallgrass, riverfront, or in the case of **Neosho National Fish Hatchery** (page 15), spawning pools. They offer road-weary travelers and their young passengers an ideal place to get out and stretch.

Controlled burn at Prairie State Park.

Prairie State Park ⑫

near Mindenmines, Missouri (128 NW 150th Lane in rural Barton County)

Park with visitor center, trails, and camping. Hours: dawn to dusk; visitor center open 10 to 4 Wednesday thru Saturday, April to October (closed Wednesday in the off-season). **Free.** Campsites must be reserved in advance. ♿: Visitor center yes; trails are unpaved. Who runs it: Missouri State Parks (mostateparks.com). ✆ 417-843-6711.

Our Take

A beautifully tended preserve of native Missouri grasses and wildflowers.

As we approached Prairie State Park on a bright, windless autumn day, the sky suddenly turned dark. We looked up to see the sun shrouded behind a red cloud of thick smoke (pictured). Looking to the horizon, we spotted the park ranger's truck and the orderly row of fire. The controlled burn is a familiar sight to Kansans who live near tallgrass prairie, which now relies on humans to do what lightning once did — burning off the woody plants that encroach on grassland. But it thrilled us to be witnessing this ritual in Missouri, on the state's largest contiguous stretch of surviving prairie.

Prairie State Park offers a glimpse of what this part of the world looked like for millions of years: a vast sea of grass and wildflowers that supplied nutrition to the bison and elk who once defined the Western landscape. Like most surviving prairies, the 3,942-acre park sits mostly atop bedrock and a thin layer of soil, making it unfit for traditional agriculture. Supported on sturdy taproots, tallgrass can grow as high as six feet or more and withstand the harshest conditions. A total of 350 native prairie plants thrive here, supporting an abundance of wildlife, including 150 species of birds, 25 species of mammals, 25 types of reptiles, and at least 112 different amphibian types.

Prairie State Park offers a variety of interlinked hiking trails, a brookside, shaded picnic area, and primitive campsites for sleeping under the stars. A staffed visitor center has nature exhibits and east-facing picture windows for prairie-gazing. Park guides offer bison hikes and wildflower hikes. In spring you may be able to spot newborn bison with their telltale orange hides.

☛ **Near here:** Harry S. Truman Birthplace, about 17 miles (page 207).

Mount Mitchell Heritage Prairie ⓫
near Wamego, Kansas (Highway K-99, 5.5 miles north of Interstate 70)

Prairie preserve with hiking trail. Hours: dawn to dusk. **Free.** ♿: No. Who maintains it: Mount Mitchell Prairie Guards. Tours and info: info@ mountmitchellprairie.org (e-mail is promptly answered).

 Our Take

Take in the Flint Hills with this scenic hiking trail on what was once an abolitionist colony.

Mount Mitchell Heritage Prairie was named after William Mitchell, leader of the anti-slavery Connecticut Kansas Colony, 63 men, women, and children who settled this area in 1856. At an organizing meeting in New Haven, the emigrants were treated to a rousing sermon by none other than Henry Ward Beecher, the "most famous man in America," the celebrated abolitionist preacher and brother of Harriet Beecher Stowe, who wrote *Uncle Tom's Cabin.*

After Beecher spoke, someone declared that the settlers should not be going to Kansas unarmed. At that, an eyewitness said, "one of the audience became aroused, and to the surprise of the rest, and even himself, called out, *I'll give a Sharps rifle.*" In the ensuing frenzy, twenty-five guns were quickly pledged to the colony — and Beecher pledged a matching gift of $625 to buy twenty-five more. He delivered the money along with a crate of Bibles and a note: "This book will be the foundation of your State. It will teach you to value your rights and inspire you to defend them."

Someone declared that the settlers should not be going to Kansas unarmed.

A legend was born. Newspapers went wild reporting on "Beecher's Bibles," embroidering the story as they went. The guns, it was said, were smuggled into Kansas in boxes marked "Bibles." Michael Stubbs, president of the Mount Mitchell Prairie Guards, told us that the rifles, in fact, "were prominently on display" and were actually brandished when the emigrants' steamboat was threatened at Lexington, Missouri.

Mitchell's son donated these 45 acres to the state historical society in the 1950s. But it wasn't until recently, when local residents bought the land and partnered with Kansas Audubon Society on a restoration plan, that the prairie began to return to its pristine state.

From the parking lot, an easy 0.6-mile walking trail takes you to the summit, a 360-degree panorama of sky with a historical marker. Early mornings are the best time to hike Mount Mitchell, especially in the hot months of summer. You will encounter just a single clump of shade trees (with picnic table) on your journey to the summit. The park is teeming with prairie plants and wildflowers that change seasonally.

☛ **Near here:** Manhattan, 12 miles by Highway 18 (see Index).

Beecher Bible and Rifle Church ❿

near Wamego, Kansas (1 mile NW of Mount Mitchell across Highway 99)

Historic church. Tours: by appointment. Call John Sumners at 785-617-1300. **Free.** ♿: Yes; enter on south side. Note: Bridge construction will impede access from some roads for most of 2013; call for directions.

 Our Take

Living relic of abolitionism is worth a stop.

During the perilous Bleeding Kansas years, colonists met for worship in homes, in tents, or outdoors. Only in 1862 was the stone building erected that came to be known as Beecher Bible and Rifle Church. Today it is a community church and meets for services at 9:45 a.m. every Sunday. Our guided tour was brief and worthwhile.

☛ **Near here:** Mount Mitchell Heritage Prairie (see above).

KU Natural History Museum ❼

Lawrence, Kansas (Dyche Hall, 1345 Jayhawk Boulevard on the University of Kansas campus; parking is in a nearby fee-based garage)

Large museum. Hours: 9 to 5 Tuesday thru Saturday, 9 to 8 Thursday, noon to 5 Sunday. Suggested donation: $5 adults, $3 seniors and youth. ♿: Yes. Who runs it: the university (naturalhistory.ku.edu). ✆ 785-864-4450.

 Our Take

This university collection of natural history artifacts is well-designed and kid-friendly, with helpful staff.

Four floors of exhibits covering millions of years of life on Earth sounds intimidating, though not as intimidating as the giant mosasaur in the lobby must have been in his day. However, from its inception over a century ago, the university's natural history collection has been tailored to the public. Today it is skillfully organized to appeal to child and adult alike.

The signature exhibit in this museum is itself a slice of history: an enormous diorama of North American mammals that was one of the most popular attractions at the Chicago World's Fair of 1893. Assembled by University of Kansas professor Lewis Lindsay Dyche, a naturalist with a talent for taxidermy, it depicts wolves, prairie dogs, bison, moose, and other creatures in action poses. After the fair, the exhibit was installed in this landmark hall and later enhanced with dioramas featuring other wildlife. Also here is Dyche's most famous stuffed animal — Comanche, the Army horse once thought to be the sole survivor of Little Big Horn.

Other exhibits in Dyche Hall include Bugtown, Explore Evolution, and The Life of the Past with the aforementioned mosasaurs. We found the staff knowledgeable and helpful in navigating the museum. Tours for students and adults are given every Saturday at 11 and 2 and by request. For younger visitors, the museum has put together several scavenger hunts, available at the front desk or for download at the museum's website.

Wildcat Glades ⑬

Conservation and Audubon Center in Joplin, Missouri (201 West Riviera Drive, south of Interstate 44 at Exit 6)

Nature center with walking trails. Hours: Trails open dawn to dusk; nature center open 9 to 5 Wednesday thru Saturday year-round, noon to 4

Silver Creek at Wildcat Glades.

Sunday from March to October. **Free.** ♿: Nature center and paved trails. ✆ 417-782-6287.

 Our Take

Rare chert bluffs are the claim to fame of this new nature center, located at the edge of the Ozarks.

Operated by Missouri Audubon and the state of Missouri, this conservation area's nature center, opened in 2007, leads into a network of trails through fishing and bird-watching spots and half the world's surviving chert glade. Inside the nature center is a modest collection of wildlife and kid's "discovery area," including a cylindrical aquarium that offers 360-degree views and a corner bird-watching station where visitors can hear many common bird songs at the press of a button.

To truly appreciate this site, however, you need to walk the trails. Crossing over Silver Creek, you enter upon some of the last remaining chert glade on the planet. More extreme than even the prairie to the west, chert glade is a desertlike environment where a layer of soil offers a scant barrier between bedrock and the elements. Only species with deep roots and large water-retaining leaves can survive. Joplin is the northernmost location for prickly pear cactus and other species native to the glade. Some of these plants are over 150 years old but remain small and stunted in their growth.

A must-see is Mother Nature's Gap on the Bluff Trail, a 40-foot split in the chert rock. Whatever you do, tread carefully on the uneven glade, especially when stepping on exposed rock.

☛ **Near here:** George Washington Carver National Monument, about 15 miles (page 191)

Neosho National Fish Hatchery's new Visitor Center.

Neosho National Fish Hatchery ⓮

Neosho, Missouri (520 East Park Street)

Working hatchery with staffed information center and aquariums with rare fish. Hours: 8 to 4:30 weekdays, 10 to 4 weekends. **Free.** ♿: Yes. Who runs it: U.S. Fish and Wildlife Service (fws.gov). ☎ 417-451-0554.

 Our Take

The nation's oldest federal fish hatchery has a unique mission, terrific visitor center, and helpful staff.

A gem in the Ozark region of southwestern Missouri is the federal system's oldest continuously operated fish hatchery. Neosho was chosen in 1888 because of its gravity-fed spring that produces 1,200 to 1,600 gallons per minute. Today, some 230,000 rainbow trout are bred annually here and sent elsewhere as stock for lakes.

The hatchery is better known for its conservation efforts, which are highlighted in its spiffy visitor center, built to LEED Gold energy efficiency standards. The most notable and strange of species nurtured here is the pallid sturgeon — a boneless, shovel-nosed wonder with a 400-million-year-old pedigree. It almost went the way of the dinosaur but is making a comeback with human help. The sightless Ozark cavefish, imperiled by pollutants and chemical runoff, is also a focus of the hatchery.

If you have children in tow, visiting here is a no-brainer. For sheer entertainment it's hard to beat the feeding frenzy outside in the trout pond. Visitors can toss pellets of food into the water and watch the trout collide hilariously in midair as they lunge for the chow.

☛ **Near here:** Wildcat Glades, about 21 miles (page 13); George Washington Carver National Monument, 14 miles (page 191).

Remington Nature Center ❶
St. Joseph, Missouri (1502 MacArthur Drive, exit 7 from Interstate 229)

Nature center with riverfront walking trails. Hours: 10 to 5 Monday thru Saturday, 1 to 5 Sunday. Admission: $3 for adults, $2 seniors, $1 youth ages 4+. &: Yes. Who runs it: City of St. Joseph. ☏ 816-271-5499.

 Our Take
Take a break here after museum-hopping in St. Joe.

Remington emphasizes the region's natural history, focusing on the river region of St. Joseph and northwest Missouri. Among the displays are a functioning beehive that can be observed safely behind glass, a replica beaver dam, a 7,000-gallon aquarium stocked with local species of fish, Indian history, and Civil War artifacts of local provenance.

Greeting you at the lobby is the life-sized model of the 10,000-year-old woolly mammoth whose bones were excavated nearby. (A mascot-sized version, named Remi, makes appearances at birthday parties held at the center.) Also notable are the paved trails outside the museum, which offer opportunities to observe bird habitats and wildflower plantings along the Missouri River.

Flint Hills Discovery Center ❾
Manhattan, Kansas (315 S. 3rd Street)

Large science and history museum. Open 10 to 8 Monday thru Thursday, 10 to 5 Friday-Saturday, noon to 5 Sunday from Memorial Day to Labor Day, closing at 5 p.m. Monday-Wednesday the rest of the year. Admission $9 adults; $7 military, students, and seniors; $4 youth 2-17. &: Yes. Who runs it: the City of Manhattan. ☏ 785-587-2726.

 Our Take

Superb new museum on the tallgrass prairie, its natural history and culture, has appeal for visitors of all ages.

Located on the westernmost edge of the Big Divide region, the Flint Hills Discovery Center, which opened in 2012, is a nicely conceived and executed museum about the largest intact tallgrass prairie in North America.

Too rocky to be farmed, these prairies were the ancestral home for huge herds of buffalo which sustained many indigenous people for thousands of years. Today, the Flint Hills provide a nutritious assortment of grasses for cattle grazing. The region has not only a distinct and diverse ecosystem but understated beauty that runs deep.

The orientation movie is a spectacle you won't want to miss. The rest of the museum is divided into six themed galleries arranged in a semi-circle. These galleries follow the history of the tallgrass prairie from the unique and powerful forces that created them to the lives of Native Peoples who lived in this region to the immigrant populations who introduced cowboys and cattle to the region.

Kids can walk through an "underground" tunnel to see how this rocky soil supports vegetation. Grownups can listen in on the

Buffalo Hunt (1844), by the renowned western painter George Catlin.

voices of Flint Hills residents today as they discuss preserving the beauty and traditions of this area. There are many interactive features to the museum — the "Auction Karaoke" kiosk is sure to be a hit with the chatterboxes in your group — and the informational displays are thorough almost to a fault. But all of this is also easy to "graze" in an hour's visit. A second-floor children's play area teaches while it entertains.

Nature Centers Around Kansas City

 Our Take
We kid-tested these outdoor oases and recommend them highly. Always check for special events on their websites before your visit.

Anita B. Gorman Discovery Center ❸
Kansas City, Missouri (4750 Troost). Open 8 to 5 weekdays and 9 to 4 first and third Saturdays. Open late some Tuesdays. Trails open dawn to dusk daily. **Free.** ♿: Yes. Who runs it: State of Missouri (mdc.mo.gov). ✆ 816-759-7300.

This attractive 10-acre oasis in the heart of Kansas City's urban core greets visitors with a replica of a long boat Lewis and Clark used — a reminder that our cities are built on top of and coexist with nature. Anita Gorman focuses on educational programs that help children and adults obtain outdoor skills in camping, hiking, wildlife watching, and growing native plants. Outdoors are winding paths, wetlands, gardens, and native plants.

Prairie Park Nature Center ❽
Lawrence, Kansas (2730 SW Harper Street). Trails open dawn to dusk; nature center 9 to 5 Tuesday thru Saturday, 1 to 4 Sunday. **Free.** ♿: Yes, including trails. Who runs it: the city (lawrenceks.org). ✆ 785-832-7980.

This 72-acre urban nature preserve includes prairie, wetlands, woodlands, and a substantial-sized lake. Inside the nature center you feel the bustling, friendly atmosphere of the place as soon as you walk through the door. There is a lot of greenery, a pond stocked with fish and turtles, nonpoisonous snakes (which make up most of the common snake species in Kansas), a bank of windows overlooking the park, and cozy nooks in which to relax, watch birds, and enjoy the scene.

A playroom with puzzles, books, a puppet stage, and child-sized eagle and butterfly wings proved irresistible to our young ones. Just past the playroom is the resident macaw, who lords over the place and deigns to say "Hello!" to you if he sees fit. (Just as likely, he will let out an ear-piercing shriek when

Mary's Lake at Prairie Park in Lawrence, Kansas.

you least expect it — but the kids adore him anyway.)

Like many of the other captive creatures here, the tropical birds of Prairie Park were abandoned by their owners. The birds of prey are either injured or were left motherless. The nature center's employees are generous with their time and expertise and conduct informal programs daily, often on demand, hauling out snakes, bugs, possum, even a young alligator for children to pet and learn about.

Locals make good use of the mile-long walking trail along Mary's Lake — as you can see, so did our grandchildren.

Ernie Miller Nature Center ❻

Olathe, Kansas (909 North Highway 7). Trails open dawn to dusk. Nature Center open 9 to 4:30 Monday thru Saturday, until 5 in the summer, closed for lunch. Sunday hours vary. **Free.** ♿: Nature Center and one trail. Who runs it: Johnson County (erniemiller.com). ☎ 913-764-7759.

One of the oldest nature centers in the area is probably also the busiest, thanks to Olathe's population boom in the decades following the park's opening in 1967. Two miles of hiking trails encircle the parking lot and nature center, where busloads of kids pour in every week for programs, camps, and special events, to gaze at the captive birds (who gaze right back) and spy on wild birds congregating at the feeder. The staff offer a slate of historical and nature programs for children, adults, and seniors ("Coffee with the Birds," a bird-watching course offered in the winter, caught our eye). Most of the programs are fee-based and advertised on the center's website.

Lakeside Nature Center ❹

Kansas City, Missouri (4701 E. Gregory Blvd., in Swope Park). Open 9 to 4 Tuesday thru Saturday, 11 to 3 Sunday; trails are open sunrise to sunset. **Free.** ♿: Nature Center and one trail. Who runs it: KC Parks & Recreation (lakesidenaturecenter.org). ✆ 816-513-8960.

Lakeside benefits from its location inside the vast 1,800-acre Swope Park, which also houses the Kansas City Zoo (6800 Zoo Drive, ✆ 816-516-5800). Inside, the nature center is a haven for animals rescued and rehabilitated but unable to return to the wild, including reptiles and birds of prey. Outside, park trails provide both challenge and reward through many types of terrain: prairie, savannah, water habitats, forests, and Bethany Falls limestone.

Martha LaFite Thompson Nature Sanctuary ❷

Liberty, Missouri (407 N. LaFrenz Road). Open 8 to 5 Monday thru Saturday. Trails open until 8 p.m. in summer. Closed Mondays from October to March. Suggested $1 donation. ♿: Interpretive Center and Bush Creek Trail. Privately operated (naturesanctuary.com). ✆ 816-781-8598.

Martha LaFite Thompson was a local naturalist who wanted to provide safe sanctuary for plants, animals, and people of all ages and ability levels. The result are these 100 serene acres of habitat, including land leased from the Missouri Department of Conservation. The Interpretive Center has exhibits, small animals, a fossil display, and a bird-watching station. Within the park are four easy-walking trails, each one about a mile in length. Pick up a map inside the Interpretive Center.

Burr Oak Woods Nature Center ❺

Blue Springs, Missouri (1401 NW Park Road, 1 mile north of I-70). Trails open 7 a.m. to 8 p.m. Tuesday thru Friday during Daylight Savings Time, closing at 6 p.m. rest of year. Nature Center open 7 to 6 Tuesday thru Fri-

Bethany Falls Limestone Trail at Burr Oak Woods, Blue Springs, Missouri.

day, 8 to 5 Saturday. **Free.** &: Nature Center, Tree Trail, and fishing dock. Who runs it: State of Missouri (mdc.mo.gov). ✆ 816-228-3766.

Confederate guerrillas were said to have hidden themselves in the rocky outcroppings of Burr Oak Woods. Even today this park has an off-the-beaten-path feel, despite being just one mile from a busy interstate. The state of Missouri acquired more than 1,000 acres of woodland in 1977 and turned it into a lush conservation area that includes 18 streams and 15 ponds, attracting numerous species of amphibians, reptiles, and songbirds. Six hiking trails include one geared to disabled users. Burr Oak Woods is a popular destination for bird watchers. In addition to various blinds on the hiking trails, the center has an indoor bird-watching area. Inside you'll find several child-friendly interactive exhibits and a quiet area to relax, watch a nature film, read a book, or stare at the fish in the 3,000-gallon aquarium.

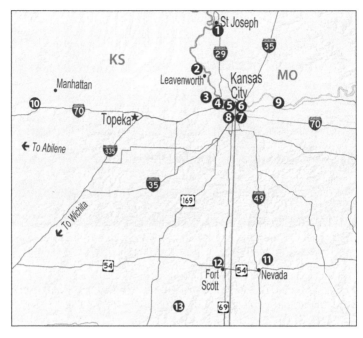

Sites in This Chapter

Tip: The Index lists all sites in every town.

Unidentified chief of the Little Osages, 1807, by
Charles de Saint-Memin.

∽ 2 ∽

First People

June 28, 1804, Captain William Clark observed, was a warm
and windy Thursday. As he sat at his writing desk, overlooking the confluence of the Missouri and Kansas rivers, Clark
was just six weeks into a two-plus-year expedition through
the American wilderness by order of President Thomas
Jefferson. This would be the third and final night that he,
Meriwether Lewis, and the Corps of Discovery would camp

at the mouth of the Kansas, a site now known as **Kaw Point** (page 30).

"This River recves its name from a nation which dwells at this time on its banks," Clark wrote in his journal. "Those Indians are not verry numerous at this time, reduced by war with their neighbors. ... I am told they are a fierce and warlike people, being badly Supplied with fire arms, become easily conquered by the Aiauway and Saukees who are better furnished with those materials of war."

The arrival of Lewis and Clark signaled the beginning of the explosive drama that would unfold along The Big Divide in the 1800s. After France sold the Indians' homeland out from under their feet — the Louisiana Purchase of 1803 — the United States used a carrot-and-stick approach to move more than a dozen tribal nations, including Kanzas, Iowas, Sacs, Missouria, and Osages, out of Missouri into present-day Kansas. Intertribal warfare was soon replaced with interracial struggle, as white missionaries, government agents, traders, and diseases converged on the Indians, putting often unbearable pressure on their numbers. The "fierce" Kanzas that Captain Clark wrote about were all but wiped out within a century, then began a tenacious comeback; today, as the Kaw Nation of Oklahoma, they are an economic and cultural success story.

Before the emigrant tribes arrived in eastern Kansas, the area had been populated by Indians for centuries. You will find arrowheads in virtually every county museum along the border. The collection in the **Wyandotte County Museum** (page 36) is especially notable. Its artifacts date back two millennia to a period when the Kansas City area was occupied by a community of Hopewell Indians, part of a chain of Hopewells that flourished across the Eastern half of North America from 200 B.C. to 500 A.D.

Less nomadic than earlier Indians, Hopewells did the kind

When the Plains Indian chiefs (from left) Young Omahaw, War Eagle, and Little Missouri came to Washington in 1821 to sign a treaty that moved them west, they posed for renowned portraitist Charles Bird King.

of things more settled-down people do, like making pottery, starting vegetable gardens, and establishing trade routes with other Hopewells. Most intriguingly, they created large earthen mounds as sacred spaces, often to bury their dead. And they left offerings at these mounds, providing an incredibly rich treasure trove for later scientists to uncover.

In 1928 an accountant named Harry Trowbridge bought a house in Kansas City, Kansas, and soon discovered it was sitting on top of a major Hopewell site. Trowbridge would spend the next three decades excavating and documenting. He became one of the world's most celebrated amateur archaeologists and would help build the Wyandotte County History Museum to share his findings with the public.

The area's other notable collections of Indian artifacts include the Kansas Museum of History, reviewed in a later chapter (page 78), and a small but well-designed gallery at the **St. Joseph Museums** (page 43). There is a large and outstanding collection of Indian textiles, pottery, and jewelry at the **Nelson-Atkins Museum** (page 44), though only a small portion is from this region.

At the time of Lewis and Clark's journey, the most formidable military and economic power in Missouri and Kansas was the Osage nation. The Osages accounted for as much as half of the continental fur trade at their peak, and had large, sustainable villages built with their wealth. Archaeological digs around the **Osage Village State Historic Site** (page 33) near Nevada, Missouri, have uncovered a developed community of some 2,000 Osages who thrived here in the 18th century.

Recognizing the need to strengthen ties to this politically astute people, Jefferson sent Clark back to Missouri in 1807 to oversee construction of **Fort Osage,** now a national landmark (page 32). Essentially a fortified trading post, it offered the Osages favorable prices on the goods they desired. Though the fur lobby eventually convinced Congress that Fort Osage was killing their business, the enterprise achieved its strategic effect of telling the world that the United States was committed to developing the lands it had acquired.

MICHAEL OVERTON

Mural of an Osage village near the settlement of fur trader (and future Confederate guerrilla) John Mathews, circa 1841. Based on a painting by E. Marie Horner of Oswego, Kansas.

Missouri was granted statehood in 1821 and promptly established trading relations with Mexico. The Mexicans' trading post in Santa Fe was a mere 900 miles from the westernmost settlements in Missouri, and soon the first wagon trains had found the way to Santa Fe. One of the most storied trade and military routes in history opened up. During the trail's 40-year heyday, thousands of heavy-laden wagons made the trip. Ruts left behind by the lumbering wagons can still be seen at points along the Santa Fe Trail. (More on this in the next chapter, "Trails West.")

Teamsters on the trails passed almost continuously through Indian lands, adding the unpredictable element of danger to an already perilous journey. Again, the government responded by building a frontier garrison. Unlike Fort Osage, however, Fort Leavenworth kept proving its worth to the country's strategic interests, and it remains an active military base to this day. The **Frontier Army Museum** (page 34) bears witness to the many roles Fort Leavenworth has played over the years.

The fort later served as headquarters for the Army of the West that invaded Mexico in 1846. Victory in the Mexican War led to the expansion of the United States to include California and New Mexico. The war also served as a training ground for many future generals of the Union and Confederate armies in the Civil War.

President Andrew Jackson signed the Indian Removal Act in 1830, forcing virtually all of America's tribal nations east of the Mississippi to uproot and resettle west of the Missouri state line. Even those Indians who had taken on European dress and manners and spouses were compelled to relocate, including the community of Wyandots from Upper Sandusky, Ohio, who gave Wyandotte County, Kansas, its name. Upon arriving in 1843, the Wyandots pitched their tents in the Missouri River bottoms. A cholera epidemic promptly wiped out one-sixth of their number. They were the first to be buried in the **Huron Indian Cemetery** (page 37**)**, which would soon develop a history of its own.

As Indians purchased and moved onto their reserves, Catholic and Protestant missionaries arrived, divvied up the tribal nations amongst themselves, and began their ministries. One of the most important and well-interpreted places in the entire region, and one of our Big Divide Top Sites, is the **Shawnee Indian Mission State Historic Site** (page 39). Its founder, a slaveholding missionary named Thomas John-

---

Tribal Nations in Eastern Kansas

In 1846 the eastern edge of Kansas looked like this. Twenty reserves were home to about 10,000 Indians, most of whom relocated here from the East after signing treaties giving up much larger reserves of land. In 1854 those treaties were ignored by the Kansas-Nebraska Act that opened up Kansas for white settlement. Most tribes were eventually relocated to present-day Oklahoma.

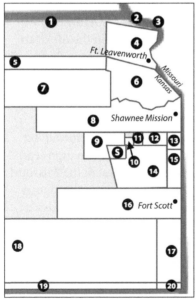

1. Otoe & Missouri
2. Iowa
3. Sac & Fox of Missouri
4. Kickapoo
5. Delaware
6. Delaware & Wyandot
7. Kansa
8. Shawnee
9. Sac & Fox of Mississippi (S=shared with Chippewa)
10. Chippewa
11. Ottawa
12. Peoria and Kaskaskia
13. Wea & Piankashaw
14. Pottawatomie
15. Miami
16. New York Indians
17. Cherokee neutral lands
18. Osage
19. Cherokee
20. Quapaw

son, would later play a key role in the pro-slavery movement in Kansas Territory.

In anticipation of Indian tribes arriving from New York State — a migration that never occurred — the

Rev. Thomas Johnson, with his wife Sarah, ran the Shawnee Indian Mission from 1830 to 1858.

government in 1842 built Fort Scott, now the **Fort Scott National Historic Site** (page 40). It enjoyed a brief heyday during the Bleeding Kansas era, when it was a pro-slavery stronghold, and the Civil War, when it became a Union Army garrison, supply depot, and useful launchpad for marauding Jayhawkers on cross-border raids. Today's Fort Scott, with 20 well-preserved buildings and parade ground, retains the look and feel of a frontier army base.

The last major military outpost built in eastern Kansas during this period was **Fort Riley** in 1853. Like the others, it was charged with peacekeeping among Indian nations and policing its portion of the frontier. But Fort Riley also played a crucial role in Border War history. Even though it is located 130 miles from the Missouri-Kansas border, it was where the very first territorial government met for a brief, tempestuous session (see First Territorial Capital State Historic Site, page 82). The story of Fort Riley — which, like Fort Leavenworth, remains an active military base — is told at the **United States Cavalry Museum** (page 42).

Lewis and Clark sculpture graces the river convergence at Kaw Point.

Kaw Point ❹

Kansas City, Kansas (Exit 423 from Interstate 70; follow signs through a large parking lot and thru a narrow "breach" in the flood wall to the park)

Riverfront park with short walking trail and monument. Hours: Open until midnight daily. **Free.** ♿: Only the 1,500-foot scenic boardwalk. Who runs it: Friends of Kaw Point (lewisandclarkwyco.org).

 Our Take

Stand at the merger of the region's two dominant rivers. Walk the circle that honors its tribal peoples.

The explorer Sieur de la Salle claimed the entire midsection of North America for King Louis XIV in 1682. For the next century, France and Spain vied for control of Louisiana Territory. But with the sale to the United States in 1803 for fifteen million dollars, or three cents per acre, the territory came into the hands of a country that desired not simply to control but to occupy the vast region.

That is what brought Lewis and Clark and the Corps of Discovery to the confluence of the Kansas and Missouri rivers on June 26, 1804. They camped here for three days before continuing their journey up the Missouri.

The government of Kansas City, Kansas, has done its best to restore a sense of the pristine beauty the explorers beheld at this six-acre park known as Kaw Point. That is no small feat given that the rivers meet at the edge of a large industrial district just off an interstate exchange. At the water's edge, this all fades away as your gaze is drawn to what is directly in front of you — a rare up-close, ground-level view of two major rivers converging.

T.A. BARNHART

The park has a short walking trail that leads up to an outdoor exhibit, where interpretive signs and a circle of marker stones pay homage to the Indian nations that were relocated into present-day Kansas in the decades after Lewis and Clark.

☛ **Near here:** "Americans by Choice" exhibit at the Dole Courthouse, about a mile (page 221); many other sites in both Kansas Citys (see Index)

Corps of Discovery Sculpture ❻
Clark's Point, Kansas City, Missouri (611 West 8th Street in Case Park)

Scenic vista with sculpture. Open daily, dawn to dusk. **Free.** ♿: Yes.

 Our Take
The most inclusive Lewis and Clark monument yet.

A high overview of the Missouri River captivated the Corps of Discovery, and their reverie is immortalized with a walkaround statue at this pocket park in Kansas City's Quality Hill neighborhood. *Corps of Discovery,* by renowned sculptor Eugene Daub, was commissioned in 2000 in advance of the Lewis and Clark bicentennial and reflects the changing perceptions of the expedition. Daub, whose statue of civil rights pioneer Rosa Parks was recently unveiled in the U.S. Capitol, may have created the most inclusive Lewis and Clark monument to date. Clark's slave York is featured, as are Sacagawea and her infant child. Even Lewis's trusty Newfoundland dog Seaman is included — a recognition, perhaps, that the audience for *Corps of Discovery* would include a lot of dog walkers who frequent city parks.

Fort Osage National Historic Landmark ❾

Sibley, Missouri (107 Osage Street; from US-24 in Buckner turn north on Sibley Road and drive 3.7 miles)

Living history replica of 1808 fort with museum and visitor center. Hours: 9 to 4:30 Tuesday thru Sunday. Admission $7 ages 14-61, $4 ages 5-13, $3 seniors. ♿: Education center and scenic overlook; staff can help with some buildings, so call ahead. Who runs it: Jackson County Parks (jacksongov.org/fortosage). ✆ 816-650-3278; press 1 for gift shop. Group tours: 816-503-4864.

 Our Take

> Kid-friendly trading post reconstructs fort life in the early 1800s along the western frontier.

The Osage empire once included large parts of Missouri, Kansas, Oklahoma, and Arkansas. Osages were a major force in the fur trade with French and American trappers and traders and were considered such a formidable military power that in 1804 President Jefferson requested a meeting with a delegation of Osage chiefs in Washington, D.C. At the summit, both nations recognized each other's strengths and vowed to become trade partners.

The Corps of Discovery camped on the north side of the Missouri River on the night of June 23, 1804. Looking across the water, Clark

Fiddler at Fort Osage.

noted a hill that offered a "high commanding position," suitable for a military fort someday. That someday came four years later, when Clark returned to oversee the opening of Fort Osage. This National Historic Landmark is a bit out of the way but is worth the drive, thanks to a dedicated staff, quality exhibits, and outstanding river views.

As you approach the site, you will see the concrete education center, built in 2007. Spend a little time inside, watching the orientation film and walking through the exhibits, before heading out the rear toward the fort. The original Fort Osage was stripped down to stone foundations soon after it closed in 1827, but this replica was painstakingly reproduced in the 1940s and 1950s from the original plans.

On-site interpreters do live demonstrations and give a flavor of what daily life was like for the 81 officers and enlisted men assigned to the fort, as well as the parade of Native Americans, traders, trappers, and civilians who came here. On a cloudy, cold weekday, there was plenty to keep our grandkids occupied; at one point an interpreter had them busy stuffing soldiers' beds with straw tick. Factor in some time to hike the easy trails down to the river.

☛ **Near here:** Independence, Missouri, about 17 miles (see Index).

Osage Village State Historic Site ⓫
Walker, Missouri (3 miles on gravel road off Highway C north of town)

Circular nature park with self-guided tour and interpretive panels. Open dawn to dusk. **Free.** ♿: Gravel path to the footbridge, beyond that rough ground. Who runs it: Missouri State Parks (mostateparks.com). Info: Call the Truman Birthplace in Lamar. ✆ 417-682-2279.

 Our Take

Informative self-guided walking tour takes you through the site of an Osage village from the 18th century.

Archaeologist Carl Chapman from the University of Missouri first surveyed this area in 1941 and confirmed that it had been a thriving Osage community through most of the 1700s. Subsequent finds revealed a village with some two hundred rectangular lodges measuring thirty to fifty feet long and fifteen to twenty feet across, laid out in streets with ceremonial space in the town center.

This serene state park is suited for leisurely walks through terrain that gently rises from the parking area. At the interpretive kiosk is a sheet of paper with a self-guided circular walking tour. From there, head up the hill to the tour stations. This is largely a nature walk through prairie grass and native plants, but will give an idea of the size of the village and how the Osages lived, hunted, farmed, and traded during the last extended period of stability in their history.

Over time the political power of the Osages would be weakened the way it was for most tribal nations — through disease and a series of confusing treaties. After relocating to Indian Territory (later known as Kansas Territory), they were removed after the Civil War to a reservation in Oklahoma.

☛ **Near here:** The Bushwhacker Museum and Jail (page 141) has artifacts from Osage Village on display.

Frontier Army Museum ❷
Fort Leavenworth, Kansas (100 Reynolds Avenue)

Large military museum. Hours: 9 to 4 Tuesday thru Friday, 10 to 4 Saturday. **Free.** ♿: Yes. Who runs it: U.S. Army Combined Arms Command (usacac.army.mil). ✆ 913-684-3767.

 Our Take
Well-stocked military museum tells story of Fort Leavenworth and the frontier Army from 1827 onward.

Today Fort Leavenworth is known for its federal penitentiary and its elite officer college, long considered the U.S. Army's intellectual center. It was here in 2006 that then-Lt. Gen. David Petraeus rewrote the counterinsurgency manual to advocate a shift in military tactics in Iraq and Afghanistan.

But the fort has served many roles over its 185-year history. Most notably, it played a crucial role in 19th-century westward expansion. Its soldiers protected the overland trails, fought in the Mexican War, and policed the western frontier after the Civil War, adding several African-American cavalry units — the Buffalo Soldiers.

Buffalo Soldiers diorama at Frontier Army Museum.

This well-curated barn of a museum draws from a collection of more than 7,000 artifacts to chronicle that history. You'll see commander Henry Leavenworth's scabbard and portrait, the giant megaphone that buglers used to blast *Reveille* before PA systems existed, a wall-sized "terrain board" that Army commanders used to plan the Battle of Chickamauga, the cannon mounted on Fort Sully (see page 173), a Curtiss airplane like the ones flown over Mexico in 1916, when the Army was looking for Pancho Villa … and on and on.

The layout is orderly and the signage good if a bit wordy. Life-size dioramas, complete with ceramic horses, are gorgeous. An acclaimed 2006 installation, *Beyond Lewis and Clark,* explains the Army's role in frontier exploration. The museum is usually not staffed, but the cell phone tour is one of the best we've used. More than a dozen short historical films are available on demand by calling the desk phone outside the theater.

☛ **ID please:** Entry to Fort Leavenworth requires a valid photo ID (driver's license or passport) of all visitors, plus vehicle inspection.

☛ **Driving tour:** Pick up the African-American driving tour brochure for directions to the Fort Sully monument. You won't need a map to find Eddie Dixon's mighty Buffalo Soldier Monument; you drive right past it on the way to the museum.

☞ **Near here:** Richard Allen Cultural Center, 2 miles (page 184); Amelia Earhart sites in Atchison (see Index), 25 miles northwest along the beautiful US-73 scenic byway

Wyandotte County Museum ➌
Bonner Springs, Kansas (631 North 126th in Wyandotte County Park)

Large, well-organized county museum. Hours: 9 to 4 weekdays year-round, 9 to noon Saturday mid-April to October. **Free.** &: Yes. Who runs it: Wyandotte County (wycomuseum.org). ✆ 913-573-5002.

 Our Take
Fascinating displays on the tribal nations who lived here in the 1800s and the Hopewells who preceded them.

This county museum is *the* place to learn about the region's indigenous population, with exhibits that are professional and eye-catching, with just the right amount of detail in their signage. The West Gallery features exhibits on the Kansas City Hopewells, part of a web of sophisticated Woodlands culture Indians that flourished from 500 B.C. to 700 A.D., and were defined by their mound-building and burial customs (even when burying their dogs). See the introduction to this chapter for more on the remarkable history behind the Wyandotte Museum.

Next to that is a gallery devoted to the tribal nations that settled in Wyandotte County: the Shawnee, Delaware, and Wyandots. Among the notable artifacts is the shotgun from "Fort Conley," set up by the Conley sisters to protect the Huron Indian Cemetery from development (see below). For the kids, there are several low-tech hands-on activities like corn grinding, a Native American language station, and pottery shard tracing. The East Gallery features the life and times of Wyandotte County.

☞ **Near here:** Grinter Place, about 9 miles (page 52); Fort Leavenworth 19 miles (see Index)

Huron Indian Cemetery

Kansas City, Kansas (North 7th and Ann)

Historic cemetery with bronze plates. Open dawn to dusk. **Free.** ♿: Only the bronze plates on 7th Street. Who runs it: Kansas Wyandots and Oklahoma Wyandottes. ✆ 913-721-1078.

💬 Our Take

This historic burial ground has a colorful story about surviving urban renewal.

The Wyandot National Burying Ground — aka Huron Indian Cemetery — is a grassy mound occupying most of a city block in downtown Kansas City, Kansas. To some it is an eyesore, to others an oasis amidst the concrete and asphalt. And to yet others the cemetery is a symbol of federal policy that wreaked needless harm on the Indian nations displaced by white settlement.

Lyda Conley and her sisters guarded their ancestors' graves, with shotgun, for two years.

Though Wyandot lawyers fought removal, they lost their court case and were forced to surrender their land in Ohio. Upon moving to their new reserve in Kansas in 1843, hundreds died in a cholera epidemic. They were the first to be buried here.

In 1855, as the government sought to take possession of Indian lands and relocate the tribal nations to present-day Oklahoma, it offered them a terrible choice: either accept U.S. citizenship and keep their existing land, or keep their tribal identity and renounce their land. Congress would try to undo the damage much later, but not before the Wyandots, Shawnees, and other nations were permanently split into two groups — those who stayed and those who left.

Thus was the stage set for the most colorful chapter in the cemetery's history: the "Fort Conley" years. In 1906 Congress authorized the Wyandotte Nation of Oklahoma to sell the Huron Cemetery to developers, a measure strongly opposed by the Wyandots of Kansas. Fearing that developers would move in before the court case was resolved, three sisters — Lyda, Helena, and Ida Conley — pitched a six-by-eight-foot shack over their ancestors' graves and guarded the cemetery day and night, with shotgun, for two years.

Meanwhile, Lyda Conley trained herself as a lawyer so she could make her case directly. She became the first Native American to argue a case before the U.S. Supreme Court. Though the Conleys lost, the publicity led Congress to repeal the earlier bill, saving the cemetery.

Eleven bronze plates at the entrance on 7th Street recount the Wyandots' 500-year history in detail, a saga aptly described as "both heroic and bitter." William Walker, a Wyandot who was the first provisional governor of the Kansas-Nebraska Territory, is buried here, as are other prominent individuals in the county's early history — and of course, all the Conleys are here, their graves impossible to miss.

In the 1990s the tribal schism flared up again, as the Oklahoma Wyandottes converted a building adjacent to the cemetery into a casino. It is quite a sight — this garish gaming facility and the ungated cemetery, cheek-to-jowl with the urban core. Someday this latest chapter will need to be recorded on a twelfth bronze plate.

☛ **Near here:** Kaw Point, about a mile (page 30); "Americans by Choice" exhibit at the Dole Courthouse, a few blocks away (page 221)

Shawnee Indian Mission
State Historic Site ❽

Fairway, Kansas (3403 West 53rd Street, near Shawnee Mission Parkway)

★ *A Big Divide Top Site* ★

Restored 1830s mission, now museum. Hours: 9 to 5 Wednesday thru Saturday. Admission: $5 adults, $1 children. ♿: East (main) building and first floor of the North building. Who runs it: Kansas Historical Society (kshs.org). ☏ 913-262-0867.

 Our Take
> Skillfully-interpreted, beautifully preserved buildings harken back to an age when Kansas was Indian country.

The Shawnee Indian Mission was founded by Rev. Thomas Johnson and his wife Sarah in response to a request for a missionary from Chief Fish, a leader of the Missouri Shawnees. The Johnsons were Methodist missionaries who came from Virginia in 1830 with their slaves. Thomas played an active role in early territorial politics. When the first territorial legislature was looking for a new place to convene after a tempestuous session in Pawnee (which we cover in a later chapter, "Border War"), Rev. Johnson agreed to let the pro-slavery delegates meet at the mission. He was eventually elected president of the so-called "bogus" legislature.

Photo mural of students, from an exhibit at Shawnee Indian Mission State Historic Site.

The historic site has long been a fixture in Johnson County (yes, it's named for him). Three of the original structures have been carefully restored and are open to visitors. A fresh interpretation in 2005 has made Shawnee Indian Mission more essential than ever, by shifting the focus from the Johnsons to the difficult lives of the young Indian children who boarded here.

Start with the first-rate video, then move to the displays, which evoke the daily life of the mission and the hardships of the students who were separated from their parents in hopes they would forget the old ways and adopt new ones. Exhibits on the second floor place the mission in the larger context of westward expansion and Bleeding Kansas politics — including an essential chart comparing the four competing constitutions, as well as displays on the Johnsons and other whites who taught here.

☞ **Related site:** Haskell Cultural Center (page 215) continues the story that begins here, as growing Indian cultural self-awareness transformed the mission school at Lawrence in the 20th century.

☞ **Near here:** Harris-Kearney House, about 4 miles (page 57); Johnson County Museum, 8 miles (page 222)

Fort Scott National Historic Site ⑫
Fort Scott, Kansas (exit US-69 at US-54)

Restored 1840s fort with extensive grounds and buildings. Hours: 8 to 5 daily April to October, 9 to 5 in the off-season. **Free.** ♿: Yes. Operated by the National Park Service (nps.gov/fosc). ✆ 620-223-0310.

 Our Take
Three museums bring to life a garrison that saw duty from the trails era through the Civil War.

Fort Scott (1842-1873) was named after Lieutenant General Winfield Scott, the 19th century's longest-serving general, whose military career spanned from the War of 1812 to the early months of the Civil War. Fort Scott was charged with peacekeeping among the tribal nations who had been resettled here and protecting traders and pioneers traveling through the region. A military road connected Fort Scott to Fort Leavenworth; today that route along Highway US-69 is designated the Frontier Military Historic Byway.

Fort Scott sent out both soldiers and dragoons (an elite corps who could fight on either foot or on horseback) to patrol the Santa Fe Trail and the Oregon Trail as far west as South Pass in Wyoming. During the Civil War, Fort Scott was a Union supply depot and a refuge for Native Americans, freedom-seeking slaves, and Missouri refugees. Confederate general Sterling Price tried and failed twice to capture the fort.

This National Historic Site consists of twenty original structures, three museums, a parade ground, and five acres of restored tallgrass prairie. Living history, interactive exhibits, and free admission add up to a great place for families seeking education and fun. The shops and eateries of downtown Fort Scott, also historic, are right next door.

☛ **Guided tours:** Offered 1 p.m. daily from Memorial Day through Labor Day. A self-guided cell phone tour is also available.

☛ **Gordon Parks:** Fort Scott is the hometown to the pioneering African-American artist Gordon Parks (page 193).

> During the Civil War, Fort Scott was a refuge for Native Americans, freedom-seeking slaves, and Missouri refugees.

☛ **Near here:** Bushwhacker Museum, about 20 miles (page 141); Mine Creek Battlefield, 23 miles (page 171)

United States Cavalry Museum ⑩
Fort Riley, Kansas (500 Huebner Road; see "ID please" note below)

Museum. Hours: 9 to 4 Monday thru Saturday, noon to 4 Sunday. **Free.** ♿: Yes. Who runs it: U.S. Cavalry Association (uscavalry.org). ✆ 785-239-2737.

 Our Take

Throwback museum uses dioramas effectively to tell the history of Fort Riley and the U.S. Cavalry.

As we entered Fort Riley for our visit to the U.S. Cavalry Museum, we saw three enormous cargo jets circling overhead. Occasionally they would disappear, then reappear. Turns out they were doing "touch-and-go" exercises at the base's Marshall Field — an oddly delicate way to describe putting 150 tons of airplane on the ground. But it did serve as a reminder of just how far this garrison had come in the 160 years since it was established by men on horseback.

While river forts like Osage and Leavenworth occupied commanding positions on bluffs, Fort Riley sat alongside the Santa Fe Trail in the central Flint Hills of Kansas. Its early years were marked, as one historian put it, by a "constant stream of people who poured through its perimeter like water through a sieve."

At first the soldiers at Fort Riley were charged with protecting westward travelers on the trail from Indian attacks. After the Civil War, they policed the western frontier and engaged the various Indian tribes, some in battle, some in friendship. George Armstrong Custer commanded the 7th Cavalry from here. Today Fort Riley serves as the permanent home of the Army's 1st Infantry Division, known as the Big Red One.

The rich history of the U.S. Cavalry, from Revolutionary War times to its demise in the 1950s, is the focus of this museum. The exhibit signage could be fresher and not so wordy, but the well-done dioramas won us over.

☛ **ID please:** Entry to Fort Riley requires a valid photo ID (driver's license or passport) of all visitors, plus vehicle inspection.

☛ **Near here:** First Territorial Capital, further down Huebner (page 82); Manhattan, 16 miles (see Index)

St. Joseph Museums ❶

St. Joseph, Missouri (3406 Frederick Avenue, west of Interstate 29 exit)

Multi-museum complex in repurposed building. Hours: 10 to 5 Monday thru Saturday, 1 to 5 Sunday. Admission $5 adults, $4 seniors, $3 youth ages 6+. &: Yes. Who runs it: Museums of St. Joseph. ℰ 800-520-8866.

 Our Take

> The Native American wing of this museum has a fine collection of artifacts from northwestern Missouri.

Among the many reasons for visiting the St. Joseph Museums complex is the Native American exhibit. It begins with a portrait gallery of over 70 Indian leaders who came to Washington, D.C., in the 1820s and 1830s, usually to sign removal treaties. There are also abundant displays of Indian jewelry, fans, moccasins, clothing and accessories, fetishes, amulets, statues, kachina dolls, and pottery. The War Room — with its tomahawks, spears, and lances — leads into the Peace Room, where dozens of peace pipes are on display. One room's fascinating exhibit illustrates the layers of an archeological dig and the artifacts that scientists would expect to find at each layer.

Display of moccasins at St. Joseph Museums.

In this and in all other exhibits in the St. Joseph Museums, the interpretive signage is concise and informative. The museum board is raising funds for a new building to replace the current one (the former State Hospital No. 2). But everything here felt fresh and compelling despite the limits of the floor plan.

☞ **There's more:** Your admission also includes the Glore Psychiatric Museum, a Big Divide Top Site (page 219), and other smaller galleries.

Nelson-Atkins Museum of Art ❼

★ *A Big Divide Top Site* ★

Kansas City, Missouri (4525 Oak)

Large world-class art gallery. Hours: 10 to 4 Wednesday, 10 to 9 Thursday-Friday, 10 to 5 Saturday, noon to 5 Sunday. **Free.** Parking in garage is $5 but free street parking is often available. ♿: Yes. Who runs it: Nelson Gallery Foundation (nelson-atkins.org). ✆ 816-751-1278.

 Our Take

One of the world's great galleries includes an impressive installation of North American Indian art.

Arikara shield, circa 1850, from
Nelson-Atkins Museum of Art.

In 2009 the Nelson-Atkins opened its newly expanded installation of North American Indian art. Seven years in the making, this 6,100-square-foot space features about 200 objects from more than 65 tribal groups in the U.S. and Canada. Though they are not the special focus of the collection, works from several of the region's emigrant tribes, including Osage, Otoe, Missouria, Wyandot, Potawatomi, and Delaware, are featured here. Critic Alice Thorson described the gallery as "one of the largest installations of American Indian art in any comprehensive museum in the world" and said it was "studded with stellar objects," such as a Hopi dress with shades of indigo "that would make painter Mark Rothko gasp."

The American Indian gallery was the vision of Marc Wilson, who as the Nelson's director for 28 years transformed every aspect of the museum en route to making it one of the premier showplaces for art in the United States. Indian art occupies but one corner of the Nelson, a vast museum that is itself a work of art, thanks to an ambitious expansion completed in 2007 by architect Steven Holl. Perched atop a sloping meadow that houses the museum's sculpture garden — as well as the giant badminton shuttlecocks by Claes Oldenburg that have become its signature pieces — the Nelson is Kansas City's greatest treasure, seen more as a public good than a private gallery. (While many taxpayer-funded sites in this guide charge admission fees, the Nelson does not.) Its vast holdings from three millennia of human creativity make the Nelson as much a history museum as an art gallery. It holds many works by Thomas Hart Benton (page 206) and George Caleb Bingham (page 150).

☞ **Be smart:** The Nelson offers a virtual docent at naguide.org with on-demand audio and written commentaries for more than 200 works in the museum, easily navigable from your smartphone or wifi device. (You can also access it from home before your visit.)

Local Museum Spotlight

Osage Mission-Neosho County Museum ⓑ

St. Paul, Kansas (203 Washington, on Highway 47). Hours: 9 to 2 Tuesday thru Saturday. **Free.** Ⓖ: Yes. Who runs it: Neosho County Historical Society (osagemission.org). Ⓒ 620-449-2320.

 Our Take

Call ahead to book a presentation and cemetery tour.

This museum is located on the site of the area's first Catholic mission. Its founder, Father John Schoenmakers, tolerated the blending of Osage spirituality and culture with Christianity. Osages make annual pilgrimages here to honor their dead and learn more about their heritage. There are no buildings from the original mission here, but the Neosho County Historical Society maintains the beautiful cemetery nearby, where many Osages, priests, and sisters of Loretto are buried and which is worth a tour. Osage Mission is also the county museum, with exhibits that include a log cabin, military uniforms, a classic car, etc. Museum volunteers can offer a short presentation on the history of the Osage Mission and a guided tour of the cemetery, with advance notice.

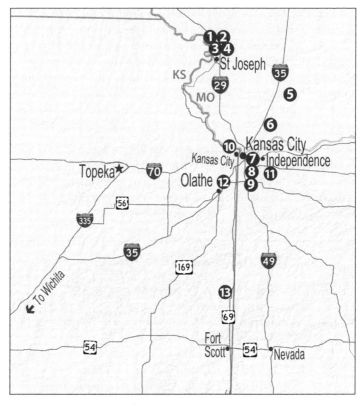

Sites in This Chapter

Tip: The Orientation Map on page 248 shows all Big Divide towns.

Conestoga wagon on the Oregon Trail.

3

Trails West

With the area west of Missouri set aside as Indian Territory, whites were permitted entry only with the approval of the U.S. Government. Moses Grinter, a young man from Kentucky, was one of those few.

Drawn to the edge of the American frontier in about 1830, Grinter apparently first set eyes on the future state of Kansas as a soldier at Cantonment Leavenworth, later Fort Leavenworth. He must have been not only hard-working but trustworthy, because the Army awarded him one of the first ferry contracts on the Kansas River. Travelers on the military road between Fort Leavenworth and Fort Gibson (in present-day Oklahoma) paid Grinter $2.00 per wagon and 50 cents per passenger to cross the river on a simple barge guided by a rope.

The ferry was on Delaware Indian land. Perhaps not surprisingly, Moses married a half-Delaware, half-white woman named Annie Marshall, who proved to be a shrewd business partner. Through his ferry receipts and their growing farming operation, they became a prosperous couple. In time they built a beautiful brick home overlooking the river, known today as **Grinter Place** (page 52).

Joseph Robidoux was another trader allowed to settle in Indian country. The American Fur Company hired him in 1826 to run a trading post north of Kansas City. Back then the Missouri state line did not follow the river, but was an invisible straight-edge border from Iowa to Arkansas. The area between that line and the Missouri River had been set aside for the Iowas, Sacs, and Foxes. But whites began encroaching on the lands and — in an all-too-familiar story — Robidoux and others started to think it might be best for all if the government removed the Indians.

In 1836, at a ceremony in Fort Leavenworth overseen by none other than William Clark, the tribal leaders agreed to take $7,500 for their land and move to new reserves across the Missouri River. The legislature moved quickly to annex the 3,100-square-mile Platte Purchase, briefly making Missouri the largest state in the Union by geographic size. Six years later, Robidoux established the city of St. Joseph, which soon became both an important trade center and a major jumping-off point for western travelers, who sometimes spent the winter at **Robidoux Row** (page 64).

Thousands of religious believers began arriving on the western border in 1830 after their prophet, Joseph Smith, received a revelation that Jackson County, Missouri, was the biblical

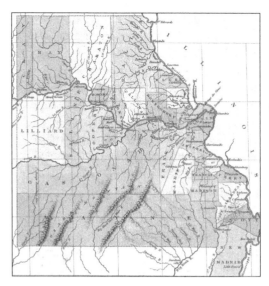
Missouri as it looked in 1827, missing the northwest corner that was annexed in 1837. West of St. Louis was largely unsettled except along the Missouri River, known as "Little Dixie" for its Southern ways that included slaveholding.

City of Zion, the site for the second coming of Christ. Smith and his followers revered Native Americans as the descendants of Adam and Eve and proselytized them (to little avail). These believers also abhorred slavery, which along with their other unusual views made them mighty suspicious to the locals. The Latter-Day Saints — as they started to call themselves during these formative years in Missouri — met strong opposition in Jackson and neighboring counties.

Eventually the Mormons, as they were also known, settled in Caldwell County and began work on a temple at **Far West** (page 55). But disputes within the church and local resistance brought these efforts to a halt in 1838. Armed hostilities broke out between Mormons and the Missouri State Guard. In response, Missouri's governor issued Executive Order No. 44 on October 27, 1838, calling for the "extermination" of all Mormons who did not promptly leave the state — which most did. Joseph Smith and five members of his inner circle were arrested and held at the **Liberty Jail** (page 53) for five months. The Saints now consider the jail a sacred place, and it is open to the public for tours.

Others used Independence and other western Missouri towns as launching points on marathon journeys across the unsettled west. Traders had charted the Santa Fe Trail in 1821; a decade later, emigrants carved out the Oregon and California trails. Still later the indefatigable Latter-Day Saints, having been chased out of Illinois after their escape from Missouri, forged the Mormon Trail to Utah. Only one museum in the country tells the stories of all four of these routes — the **National Frontier Trails Museum** (page 55), soon to undergo a major expansion. On the Kansas side, the **Mahaffie Stagecoach Stop and Farm** (page 57) offers family-friendly living history from the trail days.

By the 1850s so many people were passing through Westport in present-day Kansas City, Missouri, that a single covered-wagon outfitter serviced 11,000 outbound travelers in a single year. Small wonder that the proprietor of that shop, C. E. Kearney, was one of the first to realize the economic boon that a railroad bridge across the Missouri would bring. He led the venture to get one built, making Kansas City the region's dominant city after the Civil War. Kearney would later acquire the stately mansion, now known as the **Harris-Kearney House** (page 57), from his father-in-law John Harris, a Kentuckian who also built his fortune on pioneer traffic.

As travelers streamed through the land of the Indians, they noted the beauty of the tallgrass and the overall desirability of the land. An 1823 government map had referred to this expanse of western Plains as the "Great American Desert." This had led Easterners to assume that the territory was unfit for agriculture or even habitation. Clearly the "desert" was more fertile than these pioneers had been led to believe.

When the Kansas-Nebraska border finally opened in 1854, the Missouri River became a westward trail as well, trans-porting goods and people in such quantities that a single boat could create an instant town on the frontier. That is the

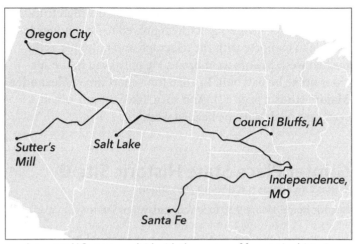

A current U.S. map overlaid with the routes of four major historic overland trails. The Oregon, California, and Santa Fe trails originated in Missouri, the Mormon route in Iowa.

premise behind one of the area's absolute must-see attractions — the **Arabia Steamboat Museum** (page 59). In 1856, the *Arabia* set off from Westport, loaded with 200 tons of cargo intended to stock a general store in a Nebraska town that existed mostly on paper. But, like hundreds of other ships in the steamboat era, the *Arabia* hit a snag and sank before reaching its destination. The people were saved, but the merchandise settled into the soft mud on the river bottom. There it lay undisturbed for 132 years until five enterprising local men dug up the boat and began restoring her treasures to their 1850s glory.

Of all the westward trails, none has evoked more romance over time than the Pony Express route. Alexander Majors, whose Santa Fe freight operation had made him wealthy, teamed with two business partners on an audacious, 1,900-mile overland trail that delivered the mail from St. Joseph to Sacramento on horseback in ten days. The **Patee House** (page 61), another of our Big Divide Top Sites, along with the **Pony Express National Museum** (page 63), tells this timeless story of risky entrepreneurship on the high frontier. Risky indeed — the Pony Express proved to be a money loser. Unable to compete with the telegraph and railroads as they pushed west, Majors went broke. He only lived in the spacious home he had built in 1856 for a short time (**Alexander Majors House,** page 62). And then, like so many others seeking a fresh start, he headed west.

Grinter Place State Historic Site ⑩

Kansas City, Kansas (1420 South 78th Street)

Historic home. Hours: 9:30 to 5 Wednesday thru Saturday. Admission: $3 adults, $1 students. ⑤: Visitor Center and first floor, plus photos of upper floor. Who runs it: Kansas Historical Society (kshs.org). ℭ 913-299-0373.

 Our Take

The oldest home in Wyandotte County is a charming, unpretentious gem of frontier building.

Moses Grinter earned a living for nearly three decades, starting in the early 1830s, floating people back and forth across the Kansas River. He married Annie Marshall, a biracial white-Delaware woman, and they had ten children, five of whom survived into adulthood. For a while, Moses ran a trading post for his in-laws, the Delawares, on whose reservation they lived. Not only did he not profit from this potential gold mine, he forgave some $14,000 in debts. Then again, you never hear a bad word spoken about the Grinters.

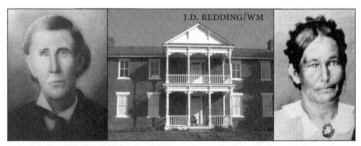

J.D. REDDING/WM

Moses Grinter, Annie Marshall Grinter, and the house they built on the Kansas River, now Grinter Place State Historic Site.

And maybe that's the real charm of Grinter Place, this home from bricks fired on-site in 1857 and overlooking the river that had secured the Grinters' future. As our tour guide took us from room to room of this tasteful yet simple showcase of 19th-century living, he told stories of a family whose greatest achievement seemed to be forging a happy home life on the frontier.

We heard of Annie's strong Methodist faith, saw the quilt squares she was stitching in later years and the pipe she smoked into old age, and learned that the dresser drawers with the edges worn off were the result of grandchildren climbing on them to get at a favorite candy jar.

The house's last private owners, Harry and Bernice Hanson, ran a popular chicken-dinner restaurant out of here until the 1960s. Mrs. Hanson finished Annie's quilt and donated that, along with the house and key artifacts, to the Kansas Historical Society. An active group of volunteers continues to create new quilts and repair old ones to support the mission of Grinter Place. The site sponsors an apple festival and "Woodside Speakers" series each year.

The visitors' center and gift shop are located in a building across the parking lot from the house. Go there when you arrive.

☛ **Near here:** Wyandotte County History Museum, about 10 miles (page 36); Shawnee Indian Mission, 14 miles (page 39)

Liberty Jail ➏
Liberty, Missouri (216 North Main Street)

Replica of historic religious place featuring dramatic storytelling. Hours: 9 to 9 daily, including holidays. **Free.** ♿: Mostly, and what isn't can be viewed from above. Who runs it: Church of Jesus Christ of Latter-Day Saints (lds.org). ✆ 816-781-3188.

 Our Take

Learn about the 1838 Mormon War, the church's exodus from Missouri, and the jailing of its leaders.

Along with Far West (see below), the ironically named Liberty Jail occupies a crucial chapter in the epic story of the Church of Jesus Christ of Latter-Day Saints. For Mormons, it is a holy site, which

Saints Driven From Jackson County Missouri,
by C. C. A. Christensen (late 1800s)

explains the spare-no-expense restoration work and a museum that's open 12 hours a day, every day. If you're comfortable with an earnest Mormon missionary as your tour guide, make time for this.

On this site the church's founding prophet, Joseph Smith, and other leaders were imprisoned in an unheated dungeon for nearly five months in the winter of 1838. Charged with treason, they languished here awaiting a trial that never came. While being transferred to another facility, the men were allowed to escape. Thus did the Saints' eight-year residency in Missouri come to an inglorious end.

Archaeologists were able to locate a portion of the original jail and build a replica using some of the recovered stones. This structure was then enclosed by a visitor center and a viewing area. Visitors can peer into a cutaway of the jail where models of the prisoners stare dejectedly at the floor, while Smith sits at a crude desk writing by candlelight. He received three revelations during his imprisonment which have become part of church doctrine. The tour presentation is skillfully enhanced, some might say overproduced, with soundtrack and soft lighting.

☞ **Near here:** Other Liberty stops are walking distance (see Index).

Far West

Temple Site in rural Caldwell County, Missouri (on Highway D)

Religious shrine of historic importance. Open 24 hours. **Free.** ♿: Yes. Info: Call the Liberty Jail site. ✆ 816-781-3188.

🗨 Our Take

More than a historical marker, this Mormon shrine is where a planned temple has been on hold for 175 years.

During the so-called "Mormon War" of 1838, Latter-Day Saints moved to Caldwell County, Missouri, to escape persecution. They planned and platted a new settlement which they called Far West, even setting the cornerstones for a temple. Today Far West is a well-tended historic park, with the 1838 cornerstones encased in glass. Three enormous stone tablets tell the story of the temple site. The church recently purchased several thousand acres of surrounding land and has an ambitious development plan for the restoration of Far West as both sacred place and tourist destination, including construction of the long-delayed temple.

National Frontier Trails Museum ⓫

Independence, Missouri (318 West Pacific)

Museum. Hours: 9 to 4:30 Monday thru Saturday, 12:30 to 4:30 p.m. Sunday. Admission: $6 adults, $5 seniors, $3 kids ages 6+. ♿: Yes. Operated by the City of Independence. ✆ 816-325-7575.

🗨 Our Take

An old favorite of ours is the only museum devoted to the history of all the overland trails.

Independence, Missouri, was the primary jumping-off point for pioneers and traders taking one of the overland trails west, so Harry Truman's hometown also serves as home to the National Frontier Trails Museum. Begin your visit by watching *West,* an award-winning 17-minute film. Through the voices of those who made the journeys, you can follow the routes taken by these pioneers. Interpretive signage, maps, artifacts, painted scenery, sun bonnets, shotguns, and covered wagons help visitors imagine the journey from hopeful beginnings to dangerous river crossings, sun-

An art gallery of trails-related works complements the historical exhibits in the National Frontier Trails Museum.

baked deserts, and treacherous mountain passes that led to what some considered the American Promised Land.

The playroom is stocked with pint-sized pioneer items. Children can also try loading a wagon with things they would need for the journey. They will quickly discover how little room there was for luxuries of any kind. A combo ticket will get you a ride on a covered wagon on days when it's operating.

☛ **Trail swales:** Across Pacific Avenue from the museum, adjacent to the Bingham-Waggoner Estate (page 152), on the far end of its parking lot is a park filled with "swales" — ruts made by the wheels of wagons that passed through this area more than 150 years ago. The short, circular trail with signage is worth the quarter-mile walk and is wheelchair accessible.

☛ **Near here:** Truman Presidential Library (page 205), Truman Home (page 207), and 1859 Jail (page 148), less than a mile

Mahaffie Stagecoach Stop and Farm ⑫

Olathe, Kansas (1200 Kansas City Road)

Living history farm with historic buildings, visitor center, and small museum. Hours: 10 to 4 Wednesday thru Saturday, noon to 4 Sunday. **Free** except special events, living history activities, and when stagecoach is running. ⓰: Yes at Heritage Center; grounds are uneven and unpaved. Who runs it: City of Olathe (olatheks.org/parksrec). ℂ 913-971-5111.

 Our Take

Excellent up-to-date living history farm for all ages.

This family-oriented site is the last stop on the Santa Fe Trail that remains open to the public. Among the original and replicated buildings here are an 1860 timbered barn, an 1865 country home, and an ice house. Depending on the time of year, you might see re-enactors spinning wool, plowing, planting, threshing, or shearing sheep. The site's working farm has horses, oxen, calves, and chickens. Most Thursdays kids can help feed the animals for $1.

Mahaffie Stagecoach Stop and Farm shows how life was lived out west, and the role of the stagecoach in westward migration. The well-appointed Heritage Center has exhibit space for special events and programs year-round. The film *Border War Voices* presents different perspectives on those who lived through the Bleeding Kansas era. Summer programming includes stagecoach rides, family nights, and living history demonstrations on blacksmithing, cooking, weaving, and other traditional crafts.

☛ **Near here:** Ernie Miller Nature Center, about 3 miles (page 19); Lanesfield School, 16 miles (page 189).

Harris-Kearney House ❽

Kansas City, Missouri (4000 Baltimore)

Historic home. Tours given: 1 to 5 Friday and Saturday, March to mid-December or by appointment. Tour fee: $6 adults. ⓰: First floor plus video tour of second floor. Who runs it: Westport Historical Society (westporthistorical.com). Info and large groups: 816-561-1821.

Recent speculation is that this portrait in the Harris-Kearney House may have been painted by George Caleb Bingham (page 150).

🗨 Our Take
Stylish home tells the story of those who stayed put and made their money off others who were moving west.

This handsome 1855 Greek Revival home is located in Westport, which is now a popular entertainment district. In pre-Civil War times, Westport was a bustling town located four miles from the steamboat dock.

Here, thousands of emigrants bought wagons and oxen and other supplies for their arduous trips west on the frontier trails. Those who could afford the expense stayed at the Harris House Hotel. John Harris, the owner, had come from Kentucky to make his fortune. As proof that he had done just that, he built this grand house with 12-foot ceilings and a hand-carved black walnut staircase. The Harris domicile was said to be the model for the house in George Caleb Bingham *Order No. 11* painting (page 150).

After Harris died in 1873, his son-in-law, railroad magnate C. E. Kearney, moved into the house and added a wing. Somehow movers jimmied the whole building onto pilings and moved it two blocks to its current location in 1922. The house passed to the Westport Historical Society in 1976, and the 1855 portion was restored to its antebellum appearance.

The Harris's 1824 Chickering square grand pianoforte is one of several eye-catching relics returned to the house by later descendants. The historical society makes Harris-Kearney its headquarters. Besides informative tours of the place, its members conduct living history demonstrations and host musical events and lectures here.

☛ **Near here:** Nelson-Atkins Museum, 1 mile (page 44), National World War I Museum, 2 miles (page 210).

Arabia Steamboat Museum ❼
Kansas City, Missouri (400 Grand Boulevard in River Market)
★ *A Big Divide Top Site* ★

Museum. Hours: Open at 10 Monday thru Saturday, noon on Sunday; closing times vary by season, but show up by 2:30 p.m. or you'll be rushing to see it all. Admission: $14.50 ages 13 to 60, $13.50 for seniors, $5.50 for kids ages 4+; group and school rates available. ♿: Yes. Who runs it: privately owned and operated (1856.com). ✆ 816-471-1856.

🗨 Our Take
Outstanding museum tells two compelling stories — a great steamboat and the quest to recover its cargo.

Is it the 1850s Walmart? An antebellum Crate & Barrel? We've heard people grasp at various retail metaphors as they tried to describe their first slack-jawed walk through the Arabia Steamboat Museum. Thousands of boots, buttons, guns, pickles, dolls, coins, perfume bottles, nails, china, on and on, pulled out of the Missouri River bottoms in the 1980s have been restored to near-mint condition and put on dazzling display.

And all because five local men employed in such industries as air conditioning and hamburgers decided to roll the dice on making a once-in-a-lifetime find — a fully loaded, sunken 19th-century riverboat.

The story behind the *Arabia's* excavation from a Kansas cornfield is as colorful as the history evoked by the cargo. Each tour begins

Dishes at the Arabia Steamboat Museum.

with a short talk and film explaining how the whole enterprise was carried out. Then you're on your own, to gaze longingly at the merchandise and wonder why no one builds stuff this nice anymore.

Wander up and down the replica deck of the *Arabia*, 171 feet long complete with paddle wheel; view the exhibits about steamboat history and culture; and observe restoration efforts that are done on-site.

☛ **Near here:** Town of Kansas Bridge, a few blocks away (page 187); National World War I Museum, about 3 miles (page 210).

Mount Mora Cemetery ❸

St. Joseph, Missouri (824 Mount Mora Road)

Historic cemetery. Open dawn to dusk. **Free.** ♿: Mausoleum Row only. Group tours available. ℂ 816-232-8471.

Mount Mora Cemetery, established in 1851, is not a national cemetery, but it is St. Joseph's oldest and most unique cemetery. Mount Mora is a who's who of the founders, pioneers, politicians, ordinary citizens, and extraordinary scoundrels who were part of St. Joseph history. Two Pony Express riders are buried here as are two of Quantrill's raiders and three governors of Missouri. Mausoleum Row at the entrance is a corridor of elaborate burial vaults for St. Joseph citizens who did not want death to keep anyone from remembering how wealthy they were. A grave finder is available to help visitors find their way around the cemetery, and group tours are available by calling the St. Joseph Museums at the above number.

 Near here: Glore Psychiatric Museum (page 219) and St. Joseph Museums (page 43), 2 miles

Patee House Museum ❷
St. Joseph, Missouri (1202 Penn Street)
★ A Big Divide Top Site ★

Large multifaceted museum. Hours: 10 to 4 Monday thru Saturday and 1 to 4 Sunday. Admission: $6 adults, $5 seniors, $4 ages 6-17. ⬥: First floor only. Who runs it: Pony Express Historical Association. ℂ 816-232-8206.

💬 Our Take
St. Joseph's most acclaimed local attraction is like a county museum on steroids.

Many museums' timelines in this part of the country are focused on the early 20th century, but St. Joe's heyday was the 1850s and 1860s, before it was eclipsed by Kansas City. Patee House fully embraces that era, with items from the Pony Express era, an 1861 stagecoach, locally fired Civil War weaponry, and beautifully restored Victorian relics.

Patee House Museum.

What really struck us about Patee House, though, was the sheer scale of *stuff* inside. This building began life in 1858 as a 140-room hotel, and those rooms, plus the corridors, are filled with exhibits. There is a one-of-a-kind carousel (which operates at limited times during the year), an 1860 train, an 1877 railroad depot, classic cars, sleighs, and a real — not replica — gallows.

The artifacts are well preserved and arranged and given simple interpretation. Its Main Street gallery of period shops and offices is one of the best we've seen, notably the dental office with equipment acquired from Walter Cronkite's father and grandfather (dentists both), and the police station with a collection of weapons used in sensational local crimes. There's a display on the local court case involving 8-foot-11 giant Robert Wadlow, dozens of regional artist George Warfel's "Westerners on Wood," and on and on.

Civil War artifacts include a Confederate Army uniform, a 38-star U.S. flag, and the restored second-floor military courtroom that was used during the war.

☛ **Near here:** Jesse James Home, next door (page 176); Pony Express Museum (page 63) and National Military Heritage Museum (page 211), less than a mile

Alexander Majors House ❾
Kansas City, Missouri (8201 State Line Road)

Historic home. Tours given 1 to 4 Saturday and Sunday or by appointment. **Free.** ♿: First floor only. Who runs it: privately operated with support from John Wornall House. ☎ 816-444-1858.

 Our Take
Tour this historically important home to learn about a founder of Kansas City and the Pony Express.

Alexander Majors was a Western trucking magnate back when trucking involved mules and oxen instead of trucks. Considered one of the founders of Kansas City, Majors is one of the three figures in a large bronze statue at the juncture of Broadway and Westport Road in Kansas City, Missouri. He was also one of the trio who founded the Pony Express. Majors was a deeply religious and temperate man who made all his employees take an oath not to drink, swear, or fight while in his employ.

Majors lived only briefly in the stately Greek Revival-style home he built in 1856. The barn on the property is a popular venue for wedding receptions and parties, but it is the house itself that is the star of the show. If it were a person, we would say it has good bones. Restored after years of neglect, the house is tastefully furnished but has few items that connect the house with Majors except for the family Bible.

Pony Express National Museum ❹
St. Joseph, Missouri (914 Penn Street)

Museum. Hours: 9 to 5 Monday thru Saturday, 1 to 5 Sunday. Admission: $6 adults, $5 seniors and youth ages 7+. ♿: Yes. Who runs it: privately operated. ☎ 816-279-5059.

 Our Take

Engaging tribute to the short-lived mail service and those who risked life and fortunes to make it happen.

At this well-done, all-ages museum, recently installed at the original stables for the Pony Express, visitors can relive one of the

Life-sized diorama of a mail rider ready to bolt out of the stable, at the Pony Express National Museum.

country's most herculean business ventures. On April 3, 1860, the first Pony Express rider left St. Joseph with a saddlebag stuffed with letters. Ten days and numerous changes of riders and horses later, the mail arrived in Sacramento, California. At the time it seemed like a miracle of communications — until, of course, the telegraph was strung along the route 18 months later.

Start with the film *A Moment in Time* in the viewing room, then move through the exhibits, including the blacksmith shop, horse stables, and rider bunkhouse, before entering the grand diorama. This 3-D timeline, stretching through the building's midsection, immerses you in the 10-day trek from Missouri to California, day by day, as the rider confronts the challenging terrains, natural elements, and other dangers, an experience enhanced with sound effects and even a heat lamp (for the desert run). A playroom lets kids act out their own version of the Pony Express.

☛ **Near here:** Robidoux Row, about 2 miles (see below); Patee House, a few blocks away (page 61)

Local Museum Spotlight

 Our Take

Both of these community museums are historically important — and packed to the gills.

Robidoux Row Museum ❶

St. Joseph, Missouri (3rd and Poulin). Hours: 1 to 4 weekends year-round except January, 1 to 4 Tuesday thru Friday in summer. Admission: $2.50 adults, $2 seniors, $1 youth 6+. ♿: Call. Who runs it: St. Joseph Historical Society. ✆ 816-232-5861.

These seven two-room apartments were built in the 1840s by fur trader Joseph Robidoux to provide temporary shelter for families awaiting new homes. They are the only surviving structures from Robidoux's years building St. Joseph into a regional trade hub. Later, he rented the apartments to pioneers who stopped to rest and restock in St. Joseph en route to the Oregon and California trails.

Located in an industrial part of town, Robidoux Row was in shambles and slated for demolition, until local advocates rescued and completely restored it. A rocking chair, cane, and timepiece are the only items in the museum that once belonged to Robidoux. The entry has a display on the role of fur trading

Robidoux Row Museum.

in developing the region. The rest of the museum is a mix of historic items with little interpretive signage.

☞ **Near here:** All the other St. Joseph sites (see Index).

Trading Post Museum ⓭
Pleasanton, Kansas (15710 North 4th Street; take the Butler exit from US-69 just east of the exchange to Valley Road). Hours: 9:30 to 4:30 Tuesday thru Saturday and 1 to 5 Sunday, April to October. Suggested donation $2.50. ♿: Yes. Who runs it: community members. ✆ 913-352-6441.

The French established Trading Post in 1838 on the Military Road from Fort Leavenworth. All that is left are a few homes and this museum of the same name — aptly named, we might add. Packed to the gills with artifacts and local treasures, the museum has a frontier feel to it, with brown and beige the dominant colors.

There is a focus on two historic events that happened nearby. One is the Marais des Cygnes Massacre in 1858 (see page 93). A large, heavy door is said to have been the entry to John Brown's "fort" near the Marais des Cygnes massacre site. The other is the Battle of Marais des Cygnes, also known as the Battle of Trading Post. Your guide may take you to the front door of the museum and point to the field where the battle took place on October 25, 1864. From here the battle moved to Mine Creek (page 171). Four of those killed at Marais des Cygnes are buried in the adjoining cemetery as is the one lucky man who escaped injury.

The museum is in a nondescript steel building. Look for proprietor Alice Widner's big friendly dog running around outside.

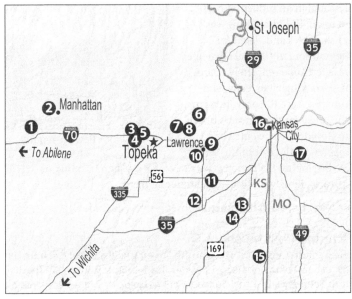

Sites in this Chapter

Tip: The Index lists all sites in every town.

1850s cartoon depicting a "Peace Convention at Fort Scott, Kansas."

4

Border War

By late 1853 it was clear that the Army's so-called "permanent Indian boundary" was going to go the way of so many other promises made to Native Americans. Running along the western border of Missouri, it was meant to keep non-Indians from squatting on the reservations that the government had set aside for the tribal nations as part of the 1830 Indian Removal Act. But travelers on the overland trails heading west were allowed to cross the boundary and pass through this territory. And many of them had taken notice of the millions of verdant acres they were passing by. As interest in the land grew, calls increased for Congress to settle its differences over slavery and open up the territory for white settlement.

Enter Stephen A. Douglas, the "Little Giant," a hard-charging, five-foot-four senator from Illinois and, in 1850, the rising star of the Democratic Party. Douglas saw the Indians' land

as a key link in the Transcontinental Railroad he dreamed of building from Chicago to the Pacific Ocean. The main impediment was the Southern voting bloc in Congress, which wanted assurances about the future survival of slavery.

The Missouri Compromise of 1820 had forged a delicate balance between pro-slavery and anti-slavery factions in Congress. It had brought Missouri into the Union as a slave state but had also

Stephen A. Douglas.

stipulated that, except in Missouri, slavery could not be practiced north of the state's southern border. The problem for Douglas was that the Indians' land lay north of that border, and could not be opened to slaveholders unless the Missouri Compromise were repealed. Many Northerners, however, had known the compromise all their lives and held it to be as sacred a text as the Constitution itself.

Passions were building on both sides. The astounding success of Harriet Beecher Stowe's 1853 novel *Uncle Tom's Cabin* (only the Bible sold more copies during the 19th century) was one of several signs that anti-slavery feeling among Northerners was growing. Meanwhile, Southern support for its "peculiar institution" was all but unanimous, even though most Southerners did not own slaves.

Unlike other slave states, Missouri was made up almost entirely of small farms, not plantations. Most Missouri slave-

This Border War-era map shows Van Buren County, Missouri, after it was renamed Cass County in retaliation for Martin Van Buren's anti-slavery views. At left, Lykins County, Kansas, was later renamed Miami County to protest Baptist missionary David Lykins's role in the pro-slavery territorial legislature. At top, Johnson County, Kansas, retained its name despite Rev. Thomas Johnson's role in the pro-slavery legislature — he sided strongly with the Union in the Civil War.

holders owned only a handful of slaves. Yet their untold thousands of hours of unpaid labor allowed these farmers to turn a profit and eventually grow prosperous. This had a powerful effect on their neighbors. Historian Jeremy Neely compared census and income records from 1850 and 1860 and found that "border settlers saw their personal wealth double and even triple" when they added slaves. As a result, "many more local households joined the class of local slave-holders and thereby demonstrated chattel bondage was expanding along, not receding from, the border."

Not surprisingly, western Missourians saw any attempt to restrict slavery as a threat to their livelihood. As a sign of how strongly they felt, residents of Van Buren County, Missouri, petitioned to have the county's name changed after former president Martin Van Buren left the Democratic Party in

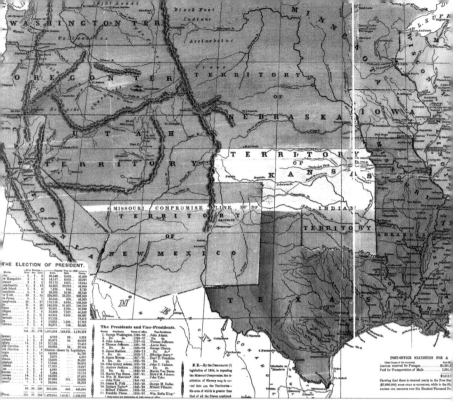

1848 to help form the anti-slavery Free Soil Party. The name was changed to Cass County, in honor of Lewis Cass, that year's Democratic candidate for president.

It was a prescient choice. Cass was a Northerner who often made common cause with Southerners, and it was his idea that Stephen Douglas would use in order to get around the Missouri Compromise. The idea was popular sovereignty. Congress would leave the question of slavery up to local voters in each territory when they petitioned to join the Union.

Douglas's thinking is easy to see when looking at the above map. Organizers were planning carve a new state known as Kansas out of the Indians' land. Kansas was adjacent to Missouri and a logical route to expand slavery. For an increasing number of western Missourians, this would also protect their

This widely circulated political map from 1856 shows Kansas Territory (unshaded) at the center of the national furor between slave states (shaded dark) and states that outlawed slavery. William C. Reynolds created the map to show that the vast territories held by the U.S. were now at risk of becoming slave states because of the 1854 repeal of the Missouri Compromise line (shown hovering over New Mexico). In reality, most Northern territories were unlikely to ratify slaveholding.

investment by making it impossible for their slaves to run across an invisible state line to freedom.

Douglas persuaded his fellow Northern Democrats to accept the proposal. "Popular sovereignty" had the ring of democracy to it, and besides, other territories were likely to counter-balance Kansas by opposing slavery when they petitioned for statehood. The appeal to Southern Democrats was obvious: Kansas, once off-limits to slaveholding, would now be theirs for the taking.

Douglas introduced his landmark bill on January 4, 1854 — the Kansas-Nebraska Act. Historians now consider it to be one of the most consequential pieces of legislation ever passed by Congress. It would be the last compromise Congress would pass before secession. In the months that followed, Kansas-Nebraska would set off a chain reaction that fractured the Union politically and ultimately ended in violence. When you hear people on The Big Divide tell you that the Civil War started here, this is what they mean.

Understanding this turning point in our nation's history is one of the primary aims of the Kansas Historical Society. Six of its sites are in this chapter, all of them essential, led by the flagship **Kansas Museum of History** in Topeka (page 78). It has a large permanent exhibit on the Bleeding Kansas period, as well as exhibits on other colorful eras in state history. A special exhibit on the Kansas-Nebraska Act that was developed for the National Archives in 2008 is now on permanent display at Lawrence's **Carnegie Building** (page 80).

At first, pro-slavery Missourians assumed that Kansas would be populated by Southerners who saw the world much the way they did. But emigrants poured into Kansas from all parts of the country, united in their desire for cheap land and not naturally inclined toward slaveholding. Within a year of the passage of the Kansas-Nebraska Act, wrote Richard Brownlee, "there had gathered along the Missouri-Kansas line men with convictions so at variance, so explosively emotional over the expansion of slavery, they dared to express them by illegal force."

David Rice Atchison, Missouri's raw-boned, rabble-rousing senator, led the pro-Southern forces. "If we win, we carry slavery to the Pacific," he thundered. Atchison upheld the right of slaveholders to defend their rights by all necessary means, including violence. Some of Missouri's most notable men supported this inflammatory rhetoric and call to arms. They included the governor, Sterling Price, the future governor, Claiborne Fox Jackson, and J.O. Shelby, a hemp farmer and one of the wealthiest slave owners in Missouri. Remember those names — they will come roaring back in later chapters on the Civil War.

With the backing of these influential men, some 5,000 Missourians — who would forever after be known as "border ruffians" — loaded their rifles, mounted their horses, and charged into Kansas to vote illegally in the first territorial elections.

To counter the Missouri threat, free-state Kansans produced their own crop of hardcore belligerents, known as Jayhawkers. They too would generate their share of household names, feared and despised by Missourians of all political persuasions: John Brown, Jim Lane, James Montgomery, Daniel Anthony (brother of Susan B.), and Charles "Doc" Jennison. The border war began in Kansas with a murder in 1855. It ended in Missouri, many years and many corpses later.

"If we win, we carry slavery to the Pacific," thundered Missouri's David Rice Atchison.

Given all this, we were a little surprised on our first visit to the living history park **Missouri Town 1855** (page 80) to find no evidence or acknowledgement anywhere that slavery existed here. Missouri Town does a laudable job of recreating antebellum life in a self-sufficient border town. It is one of our favorite places to take kids. And we appreciate the politically sensitive nature of reconstructing history with taxpayer money. Still, we think acknowledging slavery would add a necessary piece of authenticity to the site, not to mention spark some very interesting conversations.

Indeed, in 1855 the border was already a hot spot because of the slavery issue. After the fraudulent election of delegates earlier that year, Andrew Reeder — the first of ten governors sent in to tame the territory, or try anyway — ordered the opening legislative session to convene 130 miles from the border near Fort Riley (**First Territorial Capital**, page 82).

Anti-slavery settlers quickly formed a competing body to the "bogus" legislature. Led by Jim Lane, the free-state delegates convened in October 1855 in Topeka to write their own state charter and pass other laws (**Topeka Constitution Hall**, page 83). Now there were two governments in Kansas, each claiming to be the legitimate ruling power.

In time, the majority of settlers in Kansas would support the anti-slavery side for entirely pragmatic reasons. They had seen first-hand how Missouri farmers with slave labor enjoyed an unfair economic advantage. Kansas became a free state because its men believed in free, not slave, labor. Morality was a secondary concern to the Topeka legislators. In fact, these same men who voted to ban slavery in Kansas also passed a resolution that would have banned *any* African Americans, free or slave, from living and working in the new state.

Like everything else voted on in Topeka, the anti-black law lacked the authority that comes with political power. But the winds were shifting rapidly, and the storm of events that followed would reshape the political landscape.

Less than three years later, another constitutional convention would meet in Leavenworth, and those delegates not only voted to prohibit slavery in Kansas, they endorsed African-American settlement and even approved voting rights for black men. The constitution that Congress finally approved in 1861 would strike a middle ground between the Topeka and Leavenworth documents.

Meanwhile, the pro-slavery forces were firmly in charge

Free-state hellraiser Jim Lane led a joyous caravan to Constitution Hall in Lecompton in December 1857, after the anti-slavery party ticket won control of the Kansas territorial legislature. This depiction by Ellen Duncan hangs in the Territorial Capital Museum (page 96).

of the territory and enjoyed the full support of the federal government. Their capital was Lecompton, Kansas, located between the free-state strongholds of Topeka and Lawrence. Today, Lecompton is the area's leading interpreter of the Bleeding Kansas period and home to **Constitution Hall State Historic Site** (for more on Lecompton and its importance, see page 87).

The term "Bleeding Kansas" came into use in the spring of 1856 after a series of harrowing events that shocked and riveted the country. On May 21, a pro-slavery mob burned Lawrence and threw the presses of its anti-slavery paper into the Kansas River. Back in Washington Charles Sumner, a fervent abolitionist senator from Massachusetts, was delivering a blistering speech to Congress on the "rape" of Kansas by those who favored popular sovereignty. In his "Crime Against Kansas" speech, he singled out one Southern senator by name and accused him of being in love with the "harlot Slavery." The maligned senator's cousin sought out Sumner and beat him unconscious with a hard cane on the floor of the U.S. Senate. Eventually Sumner would recover — but any chance of Congressional compromise was dead.

Back in Kansas, a bloody massacre on Pottawatomie Creek introduced John Brown to the world. Brown led a posse that went to three households at night, dragged five men and boys outside, killed them with pistols and broadswords, and mutilated their bodies. Their victims' crime was support- ing the pro-slavery government, even though they were not slaveholders themselves. "The Pottawatomie killings," wrote historian Nicole Etcheson, "shattered the uneasy peace and inaugurated guerrilla war."

Brown would take part in cross-border slave raids and other guerrilla actions during his three years in Kansas Territory, stories that are told at the **John Brown Museum,** not far from the John Brown statue in Memorial Park in Osawatomie (page 89). We have also included in this chapter a survey of the artist **John Steuart Curry** (page 84), who immortalized Brown — and irritated a lot of Kansans — with his *Tragic Prelude* mural in the Kansas State Capitol.

Two weeks after the Pottawatomie Creek debacle, a small Federal force went looking for Brown, but the old man organized a band of 30 local men and ambushed them. The five hours of combat that ensued proved to be a milestone: It would be the first pitched battle anywhere between anti- slavery and pro-slavery forces — the latter, remarkably, represented by *Federal* troops. The **Black Jack Battlefield & Nature Park** (page 91), which recently received National Historic Landmark status, is an essential Bleeding Kansas stop. It hosts an annual re-enactment of the battle and tours from April to October.

Compared with the Civil War, the violence of the Border War

seems trivial — hundreds died as opposed to hundreds of thousands. But the fate of the West, and indeed the Union, hinged upon Kansas, so every violent death reverberated nationwide. Southern newspapers railed against Brown's calumny, while Northern newspapers exploded over every action against anti-slavery men.

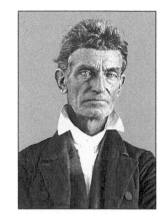

One of the most celebrated cases was the 1858 massacre at **Marais des Cygnes** (page 93), when eleven unarmed Kansans were rounded up and shot by a brigade of pro-slavery men led by Charles Hamilton — who had himself recently been removed from Kansas under threat of death by a band of Jayhawking guerrillas led by James Montgomery. It was all cause for outrage. And it all paled in comparison to the mayhem that would overwhelm the border region beginning in 1861.

"I, John Brown, am now quite certain that the crimes of this guilty land will never be purged away but with Blood."

Two emerging historic sites are devoted to telling the important but least well-documented stories of this time. These concern the people who passed through here seeking freedom from slavery. From the **Quindaro Overlook** (page 94) you can see across the Missouri River to Parkville, Missouri, and imagine a fugitive slave paddling a rickety barge on a moonless night, or chancing an escape

Wichita Indian grass lodge at Kansas Museum of History.

over the frozen river. The **Wakarusa River Valley Heritage Museum** (page 95) is dedicated to freedom seekers and those who aided them in the Lawrence-Clinton area.

Kansas Museum of History ❸

Topeka, Kansas (6425 SW 6th Avenue, exit at Wanamaker Road)

★ *A Big Divide Top Site* ★

Large multi-focus museum. Hours: 9 to 5 Tuesday thru Saturday, 1 to 5 Sunday. Admission $8 ages 6+ or $6 students with ID. ♿: Yes. Who runs it: Kansas Historical Society (kshs.org). ✆ 785-272-8681.

 Our Take

The state's official history museum is comprehensive and professionally interpreted.

Kansas Museum of History offers an expertly interpreted tour through all the chapters in the saga of Kansas, from prehistoric times to the recent past. The displays think big, from a replica of the imposing 17-foot tipi used by the Southern Cheyenne to a restored 1880 locomotive and luxury passenger car from the storied Atchison, Topeka & Santa Fe Railroad.

The curators are on staff at the Kansas Historical Society, based at the museum complex. They understand that a single well-chosen object can be more meaningful than a shelf full of objects. For instance, a display about the Oregon-California Trail features a small violin, shown in its handmade wooden case, that Irish immigrant James Limerick carried here in 1855 — a reminder that Kansas pioneers did more in their free time than just argue politics.

On the Bleeding Kansas years, the museum does not disappoint with its "Willing to Die for Freedom" gallery. The exhibit profiles four different types of emigrants (or like Limerick, immigrants), explaining each group's reasons for coming to Kansas and why people stayed despite the dangers. The exhibit also features the Indians who were here when the border opened in 1854.

The gallery on Kansas's role in the Civil War focuses on Mine Creek, the only major battle of the war fought in the state. Among the items on display are a free-state howitzer, the flag of the First Kansas Colored Volunteers Regiment, and items retrieved after Quantrill's 1863 raid on Lawrence. You even learn how many enslaved people lived in Kansas before the institution was banned.

Other permanent exhibits focus on train travel, advances in time-saving devices that revolutionized women's work, and breakthroughs in agricultural technology that made Kansas farmers the envy of the world. The low-tech interactive features of the museum are well done and include role playing and guessing the answers to historical facts.

☞ **Kids only:** Discovery Place, the museum's hands-on gallery for children, is open from 1 to 4:30 Tuesday thru Saturday or by appointment.

☞ **Near here:** Brown v. Board of Education site, about 5 miles (page 211); Kansas State Capitol, 3 miles (page 86)

Carnegie Building ➒

Lawrence, Kansas (200 West 9th Street; use Vermont Street entrance)

Interpretive panels. Open 10 to 4, Wednesday thru Friday. ♿: Yes. Who runs it: Freedom's Frontier National Heritage Area. ✆ 785-856-3040.

 Our Take
Good in-depth exhibit on Kansas-Nebraska Act is here.

The renovated Carnegie Library building has two rooms of interest: an exhibit on the Kansas-Nebraska Act, which was originally developed for the National Archives; and a room-sized timeline of the Bleeding Kansas period. The exhibits are excellent, but the timeline room can be a challenge if you do not have razor-sharp vision, as some of the signage is suspended more than 10 feet above the floor.

Missouri Town 1855 ➐

Lee's Summit, Missouri (8010 East Park Road in Fleming Park, west on Cowherd Road at 7 Highway)

Living history village. Hours: 9 to 4:30, Tuesday thru Sunday; open only on weekends mid-November to February. Admission: $5 for adults, $3 for seniors 62+ and kids 5-13. ♿: No. Who runs it: Jackson County (jackson-gov.org). ✆ 816-503-4850.

 Our Take
Well-run, family-friendly, (mostly) authentic 1850s village.

Though Missouri Town 1855 will occasionally play host to a Border War reenactment, this well-designed community is meant to evoke the customs and rituals of peaceful rural life in mid-19th-century Missouri and is set in time one year before Bleeding Kansas erupted.

Two dozen period buildings, not replicas, were hauled onto this rolling 30-acre park and restored. There's a church, school, tavern, post office, mercantile, and a variety of houses. They include that staple of Missouri plantation style, the Greek Revival home, which according to the site's lore belonged to a wealthy colonel.

The "townsfolk" are interpreters in period dress, stationed along

Missouri Town 1855 covers 30 acres that are
walkable as well as rideable.

the grounds, eager to talk to visitors about their daily lives and
demonstrate the work they do. We have been to other living-history
sites that were privately owned, and for some reason we find that
the folks here and at Fort Osage (page 32) — both run by Jackson
County's parks department — seem more "into" their roles.

Missouri Town 1855 is meant to be family-friendly, but it's also just
plain friendly. You may find yourself invited to a hymn sing-a-long
or given a chance to pet the oxen as they mosey down the lane.
Most days there is plenty to see and do — a blacksmith shaping
metal, farmers shearing sheep, musicians playing the hammered
dulcimer and other period instruments. The place teems with
activity on special event days, so plan ahead by checking the
website. Wear comfortable walking shoes.

☛ **Feeding animals:** A popular activity on the road that
approaches Missouri Town is throwing pears and apples (the only
permitted forage) over the fence to the bison, elk, and white-tailed
deer that roam the county's 110-acre Native Hooved Animal
Enclosure.

☛ **Near here:** Lone Jack Museum, about 13 miles (page 143); Burr
Oak Woods Nature Center, 10 miles (page 20)

Border War   **81**

First Territorial Capitol of Kansas ❶
Fort Riley, Kansas (692 Huebner Road; see "ID please" note below)

Historic building with exhibits. Hours: 1 to 5 Friday thru Sunday from March to October, or by appointment. Suggested donations: $3 for adults, $1 for kids. Trail open dawn to dusk. ♿: First floor only. Who runs it: Kansas Historical Society and Partners of First Territorial Capitol. ℂ 785-784-5535.

● Our Take
The struggle for Kansas began within these old stone walls, which feature informative panels and historical artifacts.

Pawnee in Kansas Territory is believed to be the shortest-lived capital city in U.S. history — less than 100 hours. Inside a stone building that was assembled so quickly that it lacked windows and doors, the first Kansas territorial legislature held a raucous session in July 1855 in which the pro-slavery majority kicked out the minority free-state delegates.

Andrew Reeder, the territory's first governor, thought that convening in Pawnee — which was near Fort Riley and about as far west as you could safely venture in those days — would insulate the government from the border chaos. But the legislature brought the chaos with them, and after four stormy days they voted to move the "capitol" back east to the Shawnee Indian Mission (page 39). The delegates who had been expelled instead went to Topeka to start their own government. The Border War had begun.

This tastefully appointed and professionally interpreted museum profiles some of the "bogus" legislators (as their opponents would begin calling them after the uproar at Pawnee). You'll also be introduced to the anti-slavery settlers who challenged them in verbal warfare that would soon become actual warfare. Upstairs, a dais and long rows of benches help you visualize the contentious scene of the first territorial assembly. Local performers occasionally descend on Pawnee to re-enact the legislative circus.

☛ **ID please:** Fort Riley is an active military base. Valid photo ID (driver's license, passport) and vehicle inspection are required.

☛ **Near here:** U.S. Cavalry Museum, about 2 miles down Huebner (page 42); Manhattan sites, 14 miles (see Index)

Dispersal of the proceedings at Topeka Constitution Hall by Federal troops on July 4, 1856, from *Frank Leslie's Illustrated Weekly*.

Topeka Constitution Hall ❺

Topeka, Kansas (429 South Kansas Avenue)

Historic building, closed for development. Supported by Friends of the Free State Capitol (constitutionalhalltopeka.com).

 Our Take

Not much to see here now, but this emerging site is historically important for two reasons.

The Topeka Constitution was written here in the fall of 1855. A couple of months later the free-state men voted to adopt the constitution and to elect Charles Robinson as governor. Now there were two competing governments in Kansas — never a good thing. President Franklin Pierce accused the leaders of the free-state movement of treason and ordered them to disband. They did not. Fearing all-out civil war, Pierce sent 400 Federal troops to disperse the Topeka legislature that was meeting here on July 4, 1856. The free-state men complied, and there was no violence — on that day. After Kansas became a state in 1861, this building served as the seat of government until the present State Capitol (page 86) could be built. Funds are being raised to develop the interior; until that happens, only the restored exterior is available for viewing.

John Steuart Curry
and the Legend of John Brown

John Steuart Curry's straightforward, accessible visions of his native state of Kansas helped define an era in American art. It was called Regionalism, and Curry, Thomas Hart Benton (page 206) and Grant Wood were the movement's triumvirate. Curry never lacked for work and he enjoyed wide acclaim during his life — except back in Kansas, where many failed to appreciate his depictions of their folkways until long after his death in 1946.

Born in 1897 in rural Jefferson County, Curry studied at the Art Institute of Chicago and worked five years as a magazine illustrator before spending a year in Paris, studying French realists

Curry in the 1930s.

and launching his career as a painter. During this time Curry realized the evocative potential of everyday life. Drawing on memories of Kansas, he was able to produce tableaus that East Coast art patrons, many of whom were unfamiliar with the ways of country folk, found both startling and engaging. Humanity, nostalgia, and strangeness blend powerfully in *Tornado in Kansas* and *Baptism in Kansas,* the two early pieces that made him famous, as well as lesser-known gems like the poignant *The Return of Private Davis from the Argonne,* which depicts a small town turning out for the funeral of one of its sons killed in World War I.

Back in Kansas, though, many people felt that Curry had deliberately chosen scenes that made them look like provincial hicks. His murals for the Kansas statehouse — particularly *Tragic Prelude* (pictured), showing a larger-than-life John Brown against the tornadoes and prairie fires, scripture in hand, his face contorted in rage — caused long-simmering resentments to boil over. The Kansas Council of Women issued a statement denouncing Curry, saying his statehouse murals "do not portray the true Kansas" but rather call attention to "the freaks in its history — the tornadoes, and John Brown, who did not follow legal procedure." Another

Detail from *Tragic Prelude* in the Kansas State Capitol in Topeka.

mural in the series, *Kansas Pastoral,* drew harrumphs from rural legislators who said Curry had not properly drawn a Hereford bull.

In time, Kansans learned to appreciate and then embrace his earnest depictions of their history and bygone culture. Don Lambert, a Kansas native and advocate for the arts, befriended Curry's widow in the 1990s and facilitated the donation of hundreds of the artist's works to Kansas State University. Eastern sophisticates had cooled to Curry and Regionalism over time, but they too came around. A national retrospective in 1998, "John Steuart Curry: Inventing the Middle West," was well-received.

Today, *Tragic Prelude* is more popular than ever, and if it has not achieved quite the iconic status of Wood's *American Gothic,* it's getting there, thanks to Photoshop and a new generation of Kansans that take pride in their unofficial state mural. (In one popular digital alteration, Brown is shown clutching the national championship trophy won by the University of Kansas men's basketball team in 2008.) Like the legend of John Brown, John Steuart Curry endures, and no historical tour of the Kansas-Missouri border region is complete without spending time face to face with his large vision.

John Steuart Curry Sites We Like

Kansas State Capitol ❹

Topeka, Kansas (10th and Jackson; underground parking on 8th Street). Open 8 to 5 weekdays, tours available 11 to 3. Capitol is open 8 to 1 Saturday for self-guided tours only. **Free.** ♿: Yes. Tours and group info: Kansas Historical Society (kshs.org). ☎ 785-296-3966.

Curry received a commission in 1936 to paint four murals and a series of panels inside the State Capitol. He did the murals first, but the hubbub they generated led the legislature to stop removal of wall tiles necessary to add new panels. Curry ceased his labors and left the murals unsigned. Today they are the highlight of the Kansas statehouse tour. The architecturally correct lamps hanging over the murals are an unfortunate impediment and cast an unwelcome light upon them. But they are still worth the trip. For a self-guided tour, download a brochure or pick one up at the Capitol.

Beach Museum of Art ❷

Manhattan, Kansas (14th and Anderson on the campus of Kansas State University). Open 10 to 5 Tuesday thru Saturday, noon to 5 Sunday. **Free.** ♿: Yes. Operated by KSU (beach.k-state.edu). ☎ 785-532-6011.

The Beach Museum's stated mission is to feature "the art of Kansas and surrounding region," and thanks to a generous gift from the artist's widow in 2002, it can claim to have more Curry works than any other museum — some 900 sketches, prints, and paintings. Most of these are too fragile to have on display, but may be viewed by appointment or on the museum's website, where its growing and impressive collection is searchable.

Curry Boyhood Home and Museum ❻

Old Jefferson Town in Oskaloosa, Kansas. Open weekend afternoons during the summer. **Free.** ♿: Yes. Info: Contact LeAnn Chapman of the Jefferson County Historical Society, ☎ 785-863–3257.

Hauled in from its original site to Old Jefferson Town (page 196), Curry's boyhood home is a gallery of originals, prints, and memorabilia. The home is only open weekends in summer, but we were able to get a guided tour in November on short notice (and without saying who we were).

Constitution Hall State Historic Site ❼

★ *A Big Divide Top Site* ★

Lecompton, Kansas (319 Elmore — just follow the signs)

Historic building with exhibits. Hours: 9 to 5 Wednesdays through Saturdays, 1 to 5 Sundays. Suggested donations: $3 adults, $1 kids. &: First floor only. Who runs it: Kansas Historical Society (kshs.org). ℰ 785-887-6520. Historic Lecompton info is at lecomptonkansas.com.

 Our Take

> Great programs and the local residents' dedication to their history make Lecompton an essential visit.

Lecompton may have placed a bet on the future of Kansas and lost, but it has recovered nicely to become a premier destination for anyone wanting to know about the Border War.

Drafted in response to the Topeka Constitution of 1855, the Lecompton Constitution was a brazen attempt to use the popular sovereignty clause of the Kansas-Nebraska Act to bring Kansas into the Union as a slave state. President James Buchanan, who supported the Lecomptonites, made them don a fig leaf of democracy to help their constitution get through Congress. So the convention voted to hold a referendum in late 1857, asking the voters of Kansas to choose between allowing the future importation of slaves or banning it. Either way they voted, however, the

Musical performance at Constitution Hall in Lecompton, Kansas.

After tearing off the hairpiece of a pro-slavery congressman, the Republican yelled, "I've scalped him!"

Lecompton Constitution would formally legalize the territory's *current* practice of slavery. As historian James McPherson put it, "Free Soilers saw this as a Heads You Win, Tails I Lose proposition." They boycotted the sham election.

Armed with their Pyrrhic victory, the pro-slavers submitted the Lecompton Constitution to Congress. A riotous debate broke out in the House of Representatives, and in one late-night session several older congressmen began throwing punches and rolling on the House floor. It broke up when a Wisconsin Republican, tearing the hairpiece from the head of a pro-slavery Democrat, declared, "I've scalped him!" to much laughter.

Buchanan was confident of victory, but the day was saved by none other than Stephen Douglas, author of the Kansas-Nebraska Act. Realizing that popular sovereignty was being thwarted by the Lecomptonites, Douglas and his allies broke with Southern Democrats and voted against a slave-state Kansas. The measure lost by eight votes in the House. In the angry aftermath that followed, the Democratic Party split into Northern and Southern factions, allowing Abraham Lincoln to win the presidency in 1860 with less than 40 percent of the popular vote. Thus did Lecompton lead to Lincoln.

The ground floor of Constitution Hall was once the U.S. Land Office, and like everything else in territorial Kansas, it was chaotic, with thousands of conflicting land claims filed here, most of them vying for unsurveyed Indian land still occupied by Indians. On the second floor things were not much better. This was where the District Court attempted to enforce the laws of the territory — another impossible task given the political climate. Fighting broke out frequently in this building and troops had to be called out from nearby Army forts to keep the peace. Small wonder that ten territorial governors passed through these doors in just seven years.

Restored to its sturdy, simple 1855 self, this example of frontier architecture now houses professionally-done exhibits and interpretive signage that help clarify the complex twists and turns of the territorial years. Check the website before visiting because special events are held both here and at Lecompton's **Territorial Capital Museum** (page 96), including a "Bleeding Kansas" lecture series in the winter.

☞ **Lecompton Reenactors:** This local group of living-history performers presents "Territorial Kansas Characters" at 2 p.m. on the first Sunday of the month during the school year at Constitution Hall. The Reenactors have been bringing to life the charged political drama of Bleeding Kansas in a town-hall setting for more than a decade.

☞ **Group packages:** Ask about a tour of Constitution Hall, the restored 1850s Democratic Headquarters, 1890s jail, and Territorial Capital Museum, with lunch and a performance by the Lecompton Reenactors.

John Brown Museum State Historic Site ⑭
Osawatomie, Kansas (10th and Main, inside Memorial Park)

Enclosed historic cabin with exhibits. Hours: 10 to 5, Tuesday through Saturday, 1 to 5 Sunday. Suggested donations of $3 for adults and $1 for kids. ⓖ: Yes. A Kansas Historic Site (kshs.org). ℂ 913-755-4384.

 Our Take
The Border War comes to life inside this cabin belonging to John Brown's sister and brother-in-law.

This small cabin was part of a loosely organized network of safe houses that made up the western edge of the Underground Railroad. Rev. Samuel Adair and his wife Florella Adair, a half-sister

The log cabin where John Brown hid after a slave raid into Missouri is protected by a stone-and-glass encasement.

to John Brown, were ardent abolitionists who welcomed Brown and a group of fugitive slaves he helped liberate during a raid in nearby Vernon County, Missouri, in which a slave owner was killed. The group spent at least one night at this cabin before continuing on an 82-day journey to freedom in Canada.

In 1928 the Adair Cabin was moved to its present location in Osawatomie's city park and encased in a stone building. The low-ceilinged cabin — watch out if you're tall! — is furnished entirely with Adair family possessions. The reed organ belonged to John Brown's daughter and was played at his funeral. There's also a spyglass once used by Brown. As with all Kansas Historical Society sites, the administrator is usually available and happy to show you around.

☛ **Near here:** Black Jack Battlefield, about 40 miles (see below); Miami County Museum, 8 miles (page 96).

Dietrich Cabin
Ottawa, Kansas (5th and Main)

Historic cabin. Hours: 1 to 4 p.m. Sundays in summer or by appointment.
Free. ♿: No. Info: Call Old Depot Museum in Ottawa ℗ 785-242-1250.

Our Take
Historically significant pioneer cabin.

Jacob and Catherine Dietrich were German immigrants who hired
out their labor to neighbors in exchange for cash to build this cabin
in 1859. They had three sons before Jacob died unexpectedly of
pneumonia in 1863. Catherine and her boys continued to live in the
cabin. To support her family she did laundry, walking six miles to
pick up the week's work and carry it home. The cabin was moved to
the center of Ottawa in 1961, the state's centennial year.

Black Jack Battlefield and Nature Park
near Baldwin City, Kansas (161 East 2000 Road, just south of US-56, 3
miles east of Baldwin City)

Battlefield with interpretive signs and walking trail. Hours: dawn to
dusk daily. Guided tours are conducted 1 p.m. weekends May to October.
Free. ♿: Rough, unpaved ground. Who runs it: Black Jack Battlefield Trust
(blackjackbattlefield.org).

Our Take
Recent recognition of this historic battle is well deserved.

In October 2012 the National Park Service designated this
battlefield a National Historic Landmark for its role in the Bleeding
Kansas saga. This designation was long-awaited vindication for the
Black Jack Battlefield Trust, the group of local stalwarts who had
fought a sometimes lonely battle for the site's recognition.

In fact, Black Jack was the opening salvo in a long and bloody war.
Visitors may be surprised to learn that the pro-slavery side was
represented by Federal forces while the anti-slavery troops were
commanded by a man wanted for murder — John Brown.

The Pottawatomie Massacre had triggered a manhunt for Brown.
"Old Osawatomie," however, evaded capture by staying on the move

Reenacting the Battle of Black Jack during the annual festival in June. "John Brown" is hiding in the trees at right.

and getting food and supplies from sympathetic supporters — a tactic that Missouri guerrillas would use during the Civil War.

A small Federal company led by Henry Clay Pate did find two of Brown's sons, however, and took them prisoner. This led to the confrontation at Black Jack. Brown's regiment, a raw cadre of anti-slavery farmers, surprised Pate's forces on the morning of June 2, 1856. Brown prevailed in the three-hour battle that ended with Pate's surrender. This victory lifted the spirits of the embattled free-state settlers, who had suffered setbacks throughout the spring.

A bronze placard has marked this woodland-and-prairie battleground for many years, but in 2004 the Black Jack Battlefield Trust purchased the 40-acre site, including an 1890s house that was built by one of Brown's company. The house has not been restored and is currently not open for tours. Every year on the Saturday closest to June 2nd, a re-enactment of the battle takes place. Other special events are held throughout the year, so check the website before traveling. Even if you can't make the events, the restored prairie area and Black Jack Nature Trail are open 365 days a year. Black Jack oaks, from which this place gets its name, grow near the stream. There are interpretive signs and a self-guided tour brochure at the picnic shelter.

☛ **Near here:** Old Depot Museum, about 20 miles (page 195); Wakarusa River Valley Heritage Museum, 27 miles (page 95)

Marais des Cygnes Massacre

State Historic Site near Pleasanton, Kansas (on East 1700 Road; exit US-69 at Highway 52 and follow signs for about 4 miles)

Outdoor historic site with interpretive signs. Hours: dawn to dusk daily. **Free.** &: Yes, if taken in from one's car. Who runs it: Kansas Historical Society (kshs.org). © 913-352-8890.

🗨 Our Take
A pristine crime scene from the Bleeding Kansas era.

In the spring of 1858, Charles Hamilton, a native of Georgia, led Missouri raiders into Linn County, Kansas, corralled eleven free-state men from nearby Trading Post, marched them into a nearby ravine, and shot them. Five men died instantly. Another five were seriously wounded, and one escaped unhurt by playing dead.

The incident was covered widely; John Greenleaf Whittier memorialized the massacre in his poem "Marais des Cygnes." One man was hanged for his role in the massacre, but Hamilton was never punished.

As you enter this historic park, a series of roadside signs tell of the disputes that led up to the Marais des Cygnes massacre. As you exit by the same road, the signs' reverse sides tell of the massacre's aftermath. From the parking area you can walk to the ditch where the victims were gunned down. Buffered by two wildlife preserves, Marais des Cygnes Massacre State Historic Site is quiet and secluded — some would even say creepy.

Detail from a diorama of the Marais des Cygnes Massacre on display at nearby Trading Post Museum (page 65).

Quindaro Overlook

Kansas City, Kansas (north of the John Brown statue at 27th and Sewell)

Outdoor pavilion with interpretive signage. Hours: dawn to dusk. **Free.** ♿: Pavilion only. Operated by the Unified Government of Wyandotte County. For more information ☎ 913-596-7077.

Our Take

Stand on the site of a unique free-state settlement for those who sought freedom on the Underground Railroad.

The Quindaro Overlook was dedicated in 2008.

The signs here tell the story of "Old Quindaro," a briefly thriving river port town whose ruins are downhill from the overlook. Quindaro was founded in 1857 to provide a safe harbor for free-soil migrants after proslavery residents blockaded all the other ports on the Missouri River. Using land purchased from local Wyandots, the town grew quickly along the steep hillside, with a population that was part Indian, part white, and part free black. Many stories have been passed down about the cooperative efforts of these three groups in the work of the Underground Railroad.

During the Civil War the town fell on hard times, but the trickle of self-emancipating slaves into this area grew into a flood. Interpretive signage in and around the pavilion relates Quindaro's historic importance to this area.

As you approach the site, note the statue of John Brown. It was erected by Western University in 1911. Originally a Freedman's School, Western University became the first historically black college west of the Mississippi. Its music school was nationally recognized, but financial difficulties caused it to close its doors in 1943.

☞ **Related site:** The nearby **Quindaro Underground Railroad**

Museum is an effort to preserve artifacts about this area's heritage. Located across from the John Brown statue, its hours are listed as 9 to 1 weekdays, but call ahead if you're interested in visiting: 913-321-1220.

☛ **Near here:** Huron Indian Cemetery, about 4 miles (page 37)

Wakarusa River Valley Heritage Museum ⑩
Clinton, Kansas (Bloomington Park East at Clinton Lake)

Museum. Hours: 1 to 5 weekends May through September, or by appointment. **Free.** ♿: Yes. Who runs it: Clinton Lake Historical Society (wakarusamuseum.org). ✆ 785-748-0800.

 Our Take
Compelling stories of an area committed to freedom in the 19th century but wiped out in the 20th.

In the 1970s Martha Parker led an effort to save the history of her township, which was about to be buried by water. The Army Corps of Engineers was building a dam to control flooding along the Wakarusa River and create a recreational area, now known as Clinton Lake. The ten communities about to be flooded into oblivion included a racially integrated village that dated back to the Border War era. It had been settled by anti-slavery settlers and free blacks.

One of the valley's notable residents was an ex-slave named George Washington who escaped from a plantation near Parkville, Missouri, into Quindaro, Kansas Territory, via local connections with the Underground Railroad. Washington was one of the soldiers in the First Kansas Colored Volunteer Infantry who fought at the Battle of Island Mound (page 146) and settled in the valley after the war.

Collecting a warehouse of memories from the communities, Parker created a museum with two missions: to preserve the memory of the lost communities and honor the families who took part in the Underground Railroad. There were many safe houses here for enslaved persons seeking freedom. As we were going to press, Parker was overseeing an expansion of the museum, which sits on a picturesque overlook on the lakefront. It will have triple the space, with new galleries and a large resource area. The museum is a little out-of-the-way but the traveler is rewarded with a commanding and scenic view of Clinton Lake. (Picnic alert!)

☛ **Near here:** Lawrence and Lecompton, both about 20 miles (see Index)

Local Museum Spotlight

 Our Take

These two community museums have artifacts of interest to any Border War or Civil War buff.

Territorial Capital Museum/Lane University ❽
Lecompton, Kansas (follow the well-placed signs). Hours: 11 to 4 Wednesday thru Saturday, 1 to 5 Sunday. **Free.** ♿: Building is retrofitted for accessibility; call ahead so staff can assist. Who runs it: Lecompton Historical Society (lecomptonkansas.com). ℂ 785-887-6148.

The U.S. Congress appropriated $50,000 to build a proper capitol for the soon-to-be state. But when Congress voted against the pro-slavery Lecompton Constitution, construction of this building stopped. Eventually it was completed and opened as a four-year school. Lane University made its own little bit of history later: Dwight D. Eisenhower's parents met and married here.

Today the building is a museum with artifacts and exhibits on three floors, including a recently acquired and restored 1890 painting of Jim Lane (namesake of the university), the desk on which the Lecompton Constitution was written, and items related to skirmishes in the area during the Border War.

Miami County Historical Museum ⓭
Paola, Kansas (12 East Peoria). Hours: 10 to 4, Monday thru Saturday. **Free.** ♿: Yes. Who runs it: Miami County Historical Society (thinkmiamicountyhistory.com). ℂ 913-294-4940.

Miami County was in the thick of things during the border battles. Abolitionist John Brown lived in Osawatomie and Missouri guerrilla William Clarke Quantrill once lived and taught school in Paola. A portrait gallery of political leaders and ordinary citizens who lived through the Bleeding Kansas era wraps around the walls of the large front room.

Another room is dedicated to military matters, including Civil War weapons, an amputation kit, and a Union jacket with two bullet holes in it from an ancestor of Miami County pioneers. Authentic Civil War jackets are not easy to come by; most old soldiers kept wearing them till they wore out. Elsewhere in the building, which was once a coffin shop, there is a gallery of wicker coffins as well as an extensive collection of Indian arrowheads, all found in the county and dating back to 10,000 B.C.

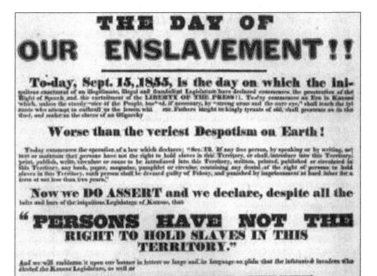

Anti-slavery opponents respond to the first territorial legislature in colorful terms on this 1855 broadside.

Civil War

With the defeat of the Lecompton Constitution, the free-state majority assumed the reins of the Kansas territorial government. In 1859 an assembly at Wyandotte City drafted yet another state constitution — with unprecedented rights for women written in — and sent it to Congress for ratification. By then, however, the continuing crisis over slavery had shifted from territories wanting to be in the Union to states that wanted out. After the election of Abraham Lincoln in 1860, seven Southern legislatures voted to secede and form the Confederate States of America (C. S. A.). The departure of their representatives from Congress cleared the way for Kansas statehood, which was ratified January 29, 1861.

Many western Missourians sympathized with the Southern cause, but years of border violence had dispelled any illusions about what they would be in for if their state joined the rebellion. Then there was the economic reality. Missourians of all political stripes depended for their livelihoods on commerce with the North. Joining the C. S. A. would put these trade relationships in jeopardy, for how long nobody could say.

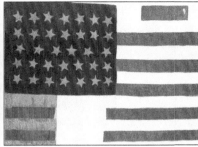

Left to right, the flags of the Confederate Army of the West, which fought at Pea Ridge; First Kansas Colored Volunteer Infantry; Sterling Price's Missouri State Guard; and the mostly German First Missouri Volunteers, which had the highest percentage of foreign-born soldiers of any regiment in the Civil War.

Though Missouri stayed in the Union, it was hardly one state indivisible. Even before the first shots were fired on Fort Sumter, a secessionist murdered his father's political rival, a Unionist, at the **Johnson County Courthouse** in Warrensburg, Missouri (page 108). Here was a new wrinkle. The Border War had been decided by strangers moving into Kansas, but the fate of Missouri in the Civil War hinged on a people who knew each other all too well.

The spark that lit this combustible mix was guerrilla warfare. John Brown's legacy of total war, on civilians as well as their armies, was carried out along the Missouri-Kansas border as nowhere else. Dozens of towns were decimated by guerrilla raids that made "Jayhawker" and "Bushwhacker" household words and gave rise to the Civil War era's most storied villains: Jim Lane, William Clarke Quantrill, Doc Jennison, the Youngers, James Montgomery, "Bloody Bill" Anderson, and Frank and Jesse James. Once Missouri was firmly under the Union Army's thumb, the situation there actually went from bad to worse. Confederate desperadoes lashed out at their Federal occupiers, who responded with brute force. Four counties east of the state line were left in smoldering ruins, and thousands of staunchly loyal Unionists were burned out along with their pro-Southern neighbors.

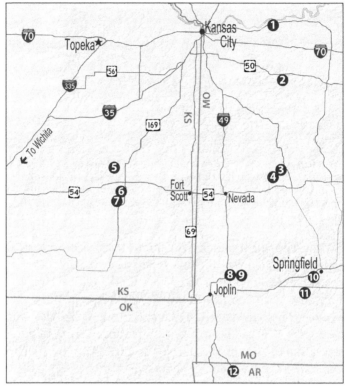

Sites in This Chapter

Tip: The Orientation Map on page 248 shows all Big Divide towns.

Gen. Nathaniel Lyon (center) is shot from his horse at Wilson's Creek, one of only two major Civil War battles fought in 1861.

✂✄ 5 ✂✄

The Battle for Missouri

Only 4 percent of Missouri's border voters cast ballots for Abraham Lincoln in the 1860 election; in Vernon and Clay counties his vote total was exactly zero. Missouri would be the only state to award all of its electoral votes to Stephen Douglas, the senator who had introduced the Kansas-Nebraska Act to appease Southern Democrats, only to oppose them on the Lecompton vote. Douglas was an unconditional Unionist — he believed secession was not an option.

101

Most Missourians agreed that secession was not the right course. Like Douglas, they believed that slavery would continue where it already existed, including Missouri. To that end they elected a governor who was both pro-Union and pro-slavery — Claiborne Fox Jackson, the onetime border ruffian and state banking commissioner. True, Jackson had participated in voter fraud and other shenanigans in Kansas Territory. By 1860, however, the Border War had died down, and Jackson was shoring up his Unionist credentials and running as a Douglas Democrat.

It turned out, though, that he was not as staunch on Unionism as advertised. In his inaugural address, the new governor stunned many in the audience by calling on Missourians "to stand by her sister slaveholding states, in whose wrongs she participates, and with whose institutions and people she sympathizes." Jackson called for a constitutional convention to deal with the secession crisis, and spent his few remaining months in office exploiting the divided loyalties of his people in an attempt to pull Missouri into the Confederacy.

After the fall of Fort Sumter in April, President Lincoln requested that governors supply him immediately with 75,000 volunteers for the Union Army. Kansans were happy to oblige; indeed, during the war the new state would enroll more volunteers in the Union Army per capita than any other. But it was a different story in states with Southern sympathies — four more legislatures voted to join the rebellion after Lincoln's decree, bringing the C. S. A. to eleven members. In Missouri, Jackson also expressed outrage at this usurpation of states' rights and urged immediate action. His constitutional delegates, who had previously voted 98 to 1 against secession, did nothing.

On April 20 a band of raiders broke into the lightly guarded Liberty Arsenal, near the present-day **Clay County Museum** in Liberty, Missouri (page 160), and made off with its contents. This caught the attention of Nathaniel Lyon, commander of the much larger St. Louis Arsenal. Lyon immediately suspected Jackson of having a hand in the Liberty Arsenal raid, and he suspected that recruits for the state militia that were drilling just outside St. Louis were actually planning a raid on his arsenal. Lyon, a born warrior who had helped Jayhawkers avoid arrest and fugitive slaves avoid capture when he was stationed at Fort Riley, Kansas, in the 1850s, turned out to be correct on both counts.

On May 9 Lyon shipped most of the munitions from his arsenal across the river to Illinois in the dead of night. The next day he led his men to the militia camp and demanded the surrender of its occupants. They were arrested without a struggle and then marched back toward the arsenal. As the prisoner parade entered downtown St. Louis, it was met by an angry mob of Confederate sympathizers. Suddenly a melee broke out and Lyon's men opened fire, killing or wounding scores of unarmed bystanders.

Missouri's new governor, who had run as a Unionist, now urged Missourians "to stand by her sister slaveholding states."

This was the provocation that Jackson had been waiting for. The next day, May 11, he pushed through the General Assembly a bill making him commander-in-chief of a new Missouri State Guard that would oppose any Union "invasion" of the state. Thousands of Missouri men rushed to sign up. Lyon, who by now had been given charge of Union forces in Missouri, confronted the governor and his military commander, Sterling Price, in a four-hour meeting in a St. Louis hotel on June 11 that ended dramatically with Lyon declaring, "This means war!"

Union forces were quickly dispersed to seize the state capital at Jefferson City and prevent the pro-Southern State Guard from gaining control of strategic outposts along the Missouri River. After a setback at the river port of Boonville, Jackson and Price decided their best option was to head to southwest Missouri and rendezvous with Ben McCulloch's Confederate forces, who were massing just across the Arkansas state line.

At Carthage, Missouri, Jackson led a ragtag army of 6,000 enthusiastic men, many armed with squirrel rifles, that drove back a detachment of Union infantry and artillery. This Confederate victory is vividly documented in art at the **Civil War Museum** (page 109) and in nature at the **Battle of Carthage State Historic Site** (page 111).

With their governor fighting battles on the run, a nervous Assembly voted to vacate Jackson's seat and reaffirm Missouri's commitment to the Union. Nonetheless, the state's southwest corner remained in play for the rest of 1861. The next and much larger engagement, on August 10 at Wilson's Creek, was one of only two major battles fought that year in the Civil War — the other being the First Battle of Bull Run — and the first to claim the life of a Union general. Lyon immediately was proclaimed a martyr in the North for his courage and uncompromising views. Nevertheless, Wilson's Creek was a decisive victory for the combined Southern forces under the commands of McCulloch and Price. It is a story expertly told at the **Wilson's Creek National Battlefield** (page 111).

Emboldened by his triumph, Price urged McCulloch to join forces with him and push back into Missouri. McCulloch was not impressed by the untrained and undisciplined State Guard and told Price that his plan was suicidal. So Price went alone, leading the guardsmen to the Union stronghold of Lexington along the Missouri River. After some initial skirmishing, Price's men laid siege to the garrison, then closed in using a brilliant and unusual strategy of moving breastworks, as you'll learn at the **Battle of Lexington State Historic Site** (page 113).

Jackson was on hand to savor that victory, but mostly he spent the fall of 1861 avoiding Federal troops. He tried holding a secession convention in Neosho, but it was hard with everybody on the run. With or without a quorum, the delegates voted to join the Confederacy, and the C.S.A. added a twelfth star to its flag. Like Kansas in the

Union Army commander Lyon declared, "This means war!"

1850s, Missouri now had rival state governments, neither of which appeared legitimate in the eyes of the other.

While this was going on, James H. Lane, the Kansas Jayhawker and politician, decided to give the Missourians a taste of the terrible new form of warfare that was to sweep over the region like prairie fire. Lane, a spellbinding orator known for his wild hair and woolly political shifts, had been a Democratic congressman from Indiana who voted for the Kansas-Nebraska Act. Upon arriving in Kansas in 1855, Lane changed horses, taking up the free-state cause with a vengeance. He devised a route ("Lane's Trail") around pro-slavery strongholds that was used by free-state settlers coming into the territory and by fugitive slaves going out.

Endlessly combative, Lane feuded almost as much with his fellow free-staters as he did with the pro-slavery forces. As the state's first U.S. senator — and by this time a Republican — Lane went to Washington in 1861 and earned President Lincoln's friendship in the days after Fort Sumter. The quick-thinking, quick-acting senator assembled a retinue of roughneck westerners who surrounded the White House and even occupied the East Room to ensure Lincoln's safety. The grateful president put Lane in charge of his own volunteer brigade. Within weeks the old Jayhawker was back in Kansas, putting together a cavalry unit to defend the border against the incursions of Sterling Price.

But Price and his Missouri State Guard were interested in Missouri, not Kansas. He engaged Lane's 600-man brigade only once, at **Dry Wood Creek** (see page 142), and rebuffed it easily. Undeterred, Lane's Brigade regrouped and then launched an invasion deep into Missouri, away from Price's army, putting the torch to any town suspected of being friendly to the Southern cause.

The raiders made it all the way to Osceola, Missouri, 60 miles from the border, where they unleashed a wild attack that killed as many as 50 men and laid waste to the entire town. If you think people there may have forgotten about Jim Lane, just visit the **Osceola Monument to Murdered Citizens** (page 115). It's one of the more vitriolic historical markers we've ever seen — and it was dedicated in 2008. Lane's belief in total war may have been radical in 1861, but it would soon become widespread. Eventually tens of thousands of non-combatants along the border would be burned out of their homes.

Jim Lane led a brigade that burned and pillaged towns in Missouri — while serving as a U.S. senator from Kansas.

A few days after Osceola, a band of Confederate irregulars rode to Humboldt, Kansas, a town that rebels had sacked six weeks earlier. This time they burned it to the ground, to shouts of "Osceola!" (**Humboldt Civil War Tour,** page 116). That battle cry would be heard again two years later during the Lawrence massacre.

Perhaps the greatest suffering in Kansas during this time was endured by a band of 9,000 Indians and some 600 of their black slaves who fled Oklahoma to avoid conscription in the Confederate Army. Pursued by rebel Indians, the fleeing Indians under the direction of the great Creek chief Opothle Yahola won two battles but were beaten in a third and forced to abandon their supplies and retreat north in the dead of winter. Though the Indians had been promised protection and supplies by Union officials, very little was done to help Opothle Yahola's band in their darkest hour. Approximately 2,000 members of these fugitives died in the most horrific conditions imaginable. Their trail of tears is remembered today at the **Opothle Yahola Memorial** in LeRoy, Kansas (page 117).

Sterling Price spent the fall of 1861 at the **Sauk River Camp** (page 116) near Osceola, raising thousands of pro-Southern recruits. But he lacked support where it counted — in Virginia, where C.S.A. President Jefferson Davis and his military strategists showed little interest in the Trans-Mississippi theater. By February, all of the bases captured by Price had been retaken by Union general Samuel R. Curtis and the newly-formed Army of the Southwest.

Curtis pushed into Arkansas, where Price and McCulloch met him at Pea Ridge. The Confederates had superior numbers, but they faltered after McCulloch was taken out by Union sharpshooters. Curtis prevailed in a battle that proved to be a game changer — a story superbly told by **Pea Ridge National Military Park** (page 119), a Class A battlefield and a Big Divide Top Site. For the rest of the war, the Union operated in Missouri from a position of strength. Price and his men were ordered east, while ex-governor Jackson fell ill and was dead by year's end.

Johnson County Historic Courthouse ❷
Warrensburg, Missouri (302 North Main Street, 1 mile west of downtown)

Historic courthouse with small museum display. Hours: 1 to 4 Monday thru Saturday. **Free.** ♿: Yes. Go next door to the Johnson County Historical Society to request entry and a tour. ✆ 660-747-6480.

 Our Take

Antebellum site saw more than its share of drama during the war and a touching story of reconciliation after.

Walking through the simple homemade exhibits on the second floor of this courthouse, which was in use from 1842 to 1871, we were struck by how many incredible stories there were from this county, which was so deeply divided *and* united that in the war's early going Union and Confederate volunteers took turns drilling on the courthouse lawn on alternating days.

There was the sensational murder that took place here on February 18, 1861. Marsh Foster, the Unionist recently elected county clerk, was killed by the son of the losing candidate, who was a secessionist. Then there was "Aunt Polly," the local woman who squirreled away all the county records on her farm for the duration of the war. And there was the young Confederate bride who used a corn cutter to fight off two Federal troops who tried to break into her house while her husband was off to war. She later went to the Union commander to demand he apologize and punish the soldiers. He did and they were.

After the war this same courthouse where divided loyalties had ended in murder was the site of a civil trial that reunited former antagonists. In a case involving two neighbors and the death of a dog named Old Drum, former Confederate George Vest — at the behest of the plaintiff's lawyer, former Union officer Wells Blodgett — delivered the "eulogy to a dog" as "man's best friend," one that has been quoted ever since. These stories and others are told inside one of the oldest buildings in the region, one that is still used today as a coffeehouse and music hall for special events.

☛ **Near here:** Confederate Memorial in Higginsville, 23 miles (page 174).

Carthage Civil War Museum ❽
Carthage, Missouri (205 South Grant, downtown)

Museum. Hours: 8:30 to 5 Tuesdays thru Saturdays, 1 to 5 Sundays. **Free.** ♿: Yes. Who runs it: the city. ✆ 417-237-7060.

 Our Take
Visit this great little museum before visiting the battle site.

The Union Army was looking to push Missouri's secessionist governor and his militia out of the state when a detachment led by Franz Sigel was disrupted by a small Confederate cavalry brigade recruited and led by Joseph O. "Jo" Shelby. Riding into the side of the Federals' line, Shelby soon had Sigel's men going backwards,

Carthage's Civil War Museum is one block from the stately
Jasper County Courthouse and square.

through the town of Carthage and to the south. But Sigel, a German
immigrant and veteran of the 1848 revolution there, kept his cool.
Over the next several hours he led an orderly withdrawal using
a maneuver he had learned in the European theater to keep his
supply train safe.

Upon entering this splendid gallery in downtown Carthage, you
are greeted by an action-packed, full-wall mural from local artist
Andy Thomas, whose work is also on display at Pea Ridge National
Military Park (page 119). Ask to see the short introductory film. It
is projected above a large diorama that will give even the logistically
challenged a clear sense of the battle, which was actually thirteen
skirmishes fought over several hours in and around town.

Throughout the room are windowbox-style exhibits on Missouri's
importance to both North and South, African Americans who
fought with the Union, Native Americans who fought with the
rebels, local legend Belle Starr, and more. On the lighter side, look
for a painting titled "Petticoat Flag," depicting a woman who has
hidden Old Glory ... well, our description won't do it justice.

☛ **Battle casualties:** Union 44 of 1,100 (4 percent), Confederate
200 of 4,000 (5 percent).

Battle of Carthage State Historic Site ❾

Carthage, Missouri (Chestnut Street at River Street)

Battlefield portion with historical marker. Hours: dawn to dusk daily. **Free.** ♿: Gravel path leads to interpretive signage. Who runs it: the state of Missouri (mostateparks.com), via the Truman Birthplace site in Lamar (☏ 417-682-2279).

 Our Take

Lovely pocket park with vivid snapshot of the action.

The Battle of Carthage stretched over ten miles, of which just a sliver at the edge of town has been preserved as a state park. It is a useful sliver, for it clearly shows the commanding position from which Franz Sigel, the retreating Union officer, directed his artillery to fire upon the Missouri State Guard troops who were in hot pursuit of his army. The fusillade kept the enemy at bay until nightfall, when Sigel's men made it back to safety.

We were beguiled by this little pocket park, with its small creek and limestone caves, on a tranquil fall afternoon. However, the on-site signage is wordy and hard to follow, so visit the downtown museum first (see above).

Wilson's Creek National Battlefield ⓫

★ *A Big Divide Top Site* ★

Republic, Missouri (6424 West Farm Road 182, 14 miles SW of Springfield)

Large battlefield with visitor center. Hours: 8 to 5 daily; battlefield is open until 9 p.m. in summer. Admission: $5 ages 16+ or $10 per car; free for kids and educational groups. Tickets good for 7 days. ♿: Yes. Who runs it: National Park Service (nps.gov/wicr). ☏ 417-732-2662, ext. 227.

 Our Take

A first-rate battlefield site with interpretation to match.

Other than the First Battle of Bull Run, 1861 was notable in Civil War history for the Battle of Wilson's Creek, the first major engagement in the Trans-Mississippi region. General Nathaniel Lyon insisted on throwing his 5,400 Union soldiers at the armies of

Reenactors during the filming of *August Light,* a new visitor center documentary, at Wilson's Creek National Battlefield.

12,000 under Price and McCulloch. After Lyon was killed, Major Samuel Sturgis assumed control of the Union, leading troops back to Springfield, their supplies low and morale lower. The victory on August 10, 1861 — shared ever-so-briefly by brigadier generals Sterling Price and Ben McCulloch — gave the Confederacy a toehold in southwestern Missouri.

Because of its strategic importance, it is one of three Big Divide battlefields rated Class A by the 1993 federal advisory committee on Civil War sites. The Wilson's Creek visitor center was being reworked during our visit, but we liked what we saw, especially the multimedia diorama.

The battlefield is well interpreted and makes for a pleasant five-mile drive or walk. Be sure to use the cell phone audio tour along the trail. It has stories worth hearing, especially about the Ray House, which served as a field hospital while family members — including their black "nanny" — crouched in the basement. Call ahead to see if the house will be open when you visit.

☛ **Battle casualties:** Union 1,317 of 5,400 (24 percent), Confederate 1,232 of 12,000 (10 percent).

Springfield National Cemetery ➓

Springfield, Missouri (1702 E. Seminole Street)

Military cemetery. Hours: dawn to dusk; office open 8 to 4:30 weekdays. **Free.** ♿: Some paved areas. Who maintains it: Department of Veterans Affairs (grave locator on-site and at cem.va.gov). ☎ 417-881-9499.

 Our Take

A beautiful, lasting reminder of the divisiveness of the war.

This austere burial ground is an oasis of serenity, a mini-Arlington in the middle of Springfield's suburban sprawl. It was established in 1867, and many soldiers who died 14 miles away at Wilson's Creek were eventually disinterred from their original graves and reburied here. One Union Army nurse, Malinda A. Moon, is interred in a place of honor at Plot 1, Grave 1-A. Nearly half of the initial Union graves were for unknown soldiers. Springfield eventually interred Confederate soldiers' remains as well, though the funds for that had to be raised privately. Those graves are located behind a stone wall and large portico that keep the two sides divided even in peace (see photo, page 163).

Battle of Lexington State Historic Site ➊

Lexington, Missouri (1101 Delaware)

Historic home and battlefield with visitor center. Hours: 9 to 5 Tuesday thru Saturday, 10 to 5 Sunday, March to October; closed Tuesdays in off-season. **Free.** Tours of Anderson House are $4 for ages 13+ and $2.50 for ages 6-12; call ahead to check on tour times. ♿: Visitor center and first floor of Anderson House. Who runs it: state of Missouri (mostateparks.com). ☎ 660-259-4654.

 Our Take

Restored battlefield and historic house ably document the ingenious rebel victory at Lexington.

After his victory at Wilson's Creek, Sterling Price marched a 12,000-man army of Missouri State Guard and other irregulars north to Lexington. Strategically located at the head of the Missouri River Valley, Lexington was the fifth largest city in the state and had

Missouri's largest slave population. To control the area, the Union army established a heavily fortified garrison under the command of Colonel James Mulligan.

Price attacked on September 13. He thought his superior numbers could overwhelm the garrison, but fighting bogged down in Machpelah Cemetery. With ammunition running low, Price decided to lay siege to the fort and await his supply train.

Damage to the Anderson House from the Battle of Lexington.

A week passed. Conditions inside the Union garrison grew desperate as thirsty troops were cut off from any water source. Finally, pro-Southern troops took bales of hemp to the river and soaked them. The next morning they pushed the soggy breastworks up the bluffs, foiling the Union cannon that poured searing fire into them. Harris' men were able to capture the artillery positions, and by noon it was all over.

After Mulligan's men surrendered their arms, Price ordered them to form a line, whereupon Governor Jackson himself appeared and, according to a report, "addressed them in harsh language, demanding what business they had to wage war in the State of Missouri, adding that when Missouri needed troops from Illinois she would ask for them."

The Visitor Center has an orientation film that by our standards is quite long, 45 minutes, but also quite good. The small museum has a diorama of the battle and other exhibits related to the battle. The battlefield is open for walking tours. For a fee you can also tour the Greek Revival Anderson House, which changed hands three times during the battle and was heavily damaged. Check the website for upcoming tours of historic Machpelah Cemetery.

☞ **Battle casualties:** Union 159 out of 3,500 (5 percent), Confederate 97 out of 12,000 (0.8 percent).

Monument to Murdered Citizens ❸

Osceola, Missouri (located in Osceola Cemetery on State Hwy WW, which loops through town from Highway 82)

Monument. Cemetery open dawn to dusk. **Free.** ♿: Brick pavers at memorial. Info: Call St. Clair County Historical Society (☎ 417-876-3925).

 Our Take

Strongly-worded memorial for an 1861 attack on the town.

With Abraham Lincoln's blessing, Jim Lane formed a 600-man brigade in Fort Scott, Kansas, in the fall of 1861 and rode across the border to terrorize Missourians. Lane's Brigade went on a rampage through Cass and Bates counties, burning and pillaging towns suspected of being rebel-friendly. Incredibly, Lane did all this while remaining a sitting U.S. senator.

The wrecking crew rode into St. Clair County and descended on Osceola, a town strategically located near two rivers (see **Sauk River Camp**, below). Osceola also had many wealthy households, including one belonging to a Senate colleague of Lane's, Waldo Johnson.

Over the next few hours, all but three buildings in town were burned. The raiders killed at least 10 men and as many as 50, and made off with whatever could be piled on wagons, including (it was said) silk dresses and a piano. Dozens of enslaved people followed the unruly brigade back to Kansas.

Back in Washington, Lane's superiors in the Union Army were appalled by the reports from Missouri. "A few more such raids will make this State unanimous against us," lamented Gen. Henry Halleck. But the president continued to tolerate Lane, whose political skills and toughness he admired.

A monument to the attack on Osceola was erected in 2008 by the Sons of Confederate Veterans and St. Clair County Historical Society. Located in a cemetery south of town, it includes a long inscription that reads in part, "This monument is dedicated to the men and women, known and unknown, who were robbed, brutalized and murdered by Union Gen. James H. Lane through the events he set in motion."

Sauk River Camp ❹

near Osceola, Missouri (1 mile SW of town on Highway 82)

Historical marker and ideal picnic site. Free. ♿: Rough ground. Info: St. Clair County Historical Society (✆ 417-876-3925).

 ## Our Take

Another reason to take the scenic drive to Osceola.

This overlook at the confluence of the Sac and Osage rivers was built by the Civilian Conservation Corps (CCC) in the 1930s, and completes a scenic drive along Highway 82 from El Dorado Springs. It offers a pleasing view of the lowlands where, as an impressive granite marker here notes, Gen. Sterling Price held camp in late 1861 for the purpose of recruiting men to the C.S.A. and Missouri State Guard. A shady picnic site overlooks this river view. You can fill your basket at Osceola Cheese on Highway 13. (We recommend anything with hot pepper.)

Humboldt Civil War Tour ❻

Humboldt, Kansas (start at the city park at Ninth and Bridge)

Self-guided driving tour. Free. Pick up a map at City Hall or local businesses like Johnson's General Store, 218 North 9th. ♿: Yes. Guided tours are available, but call ahead. ✆ 620-473-2325.

 ## Our Take

Creative self-guided tour uses etched marker stones to tell the story of rebels burning the town in 1861.

Humboldt, with just 100 residents in 1861, was attacked twice in a six-week period in retribution for its support of the Union. The first raid was led by John Mathews, a Southern-sympathizing Kansan who lived nearby and ran a trading post for local tribes. He also worked among the Indians as a recruiter for the Confederate Army. On September 8 Mathews brought some of his recruits to raid Humboldt. No one was killed but a number of homes were looted, and some escaped slaves who had found refuge in town were rounded up and returned to Missouri.

A posse soon hunted down and killed Mathews, and a home guard was established to protect Humboldt from future attacks. But it was not in place by the time of the second attack on October 14. This one was led by Missourians who were avenging not only the death of Mathews but the recent attack on Osceola. One man was shot dead and the whole town was put to the torch. From then on, Humboldt was under heavy guard for the rest of the war.

This is an easy walking or driving tour that will take you to twelve concise waist-high stone monuments, donated by the local cement factory. Bob Cross, a longtime local art teacher, designed the etchings on the stones. They reflect how residents responded in real time to the sacking of their town.

"Confederate soldier was shot here Oct. 14, 1861, as he tried to remove Union flag," reads this illustrated marker along the Humboldt Civil War Tour.

☛ **Near here:** Humboldt Historical Museum (page 121).

Opothle Yahola Memorial ❺
LeRoy, Kansas (in the city park on Main Street north of Highway 58)

Historical marker. Open dawn to dusk. **Free.** ♿: Yes. Info: Call Coffey County Library across from the memorial at 725 Main, ☏ 620-964-2321.

 Our Take

> Overdue tribute to Unionist Indians who suffered mightily in the Civil War also sheds light on their black slaves.

Near this site in LeRoy, Kansas, on May 22, 1862, the first regiment of Indian Home Guard for the Union Army was formed. It included 1,000 Indians who had gone through hell just getting there.

From their homes in present-day Oklahoma, many Creeks and Seminoles had spent 1861 trying to stay neutral in the Civil War. In November a Confederate commander came to the plantation of the Creek chief, Opothle Yahola, and demanded that his people choose sides. Opothle Yahola, who had no interest in joining the rebel army, led 9,000 Indians north on a march to Kansas, where Union officials had offered them refuge. Among their ranks were black slaves who were promised freedom in exchange for their support.

Opothle Yahola had endured the Creeks' forced removal from Georgia in 1834, but the suffering on this relatively short journey to Kansas would be far worse. About 2,000 people died from the cold, disease, and attacks by rebel forces. Exhausted and starving, the survivors limped into Fort Row, Kansas, only to find little of the support that had been promised them.

Opothle Yahola, painted in the 1830s by Charles Bird King.

Three Indian Home Guard regiments would be formed in 1862, as well as some of the first African American units to see combat in the Civil War. The Third Indian Home Guard marched on Newtonia (page 144) and battled other Indians who had chosen to fight for the Confederacy. By this time, Opothle Yahola was sitting miserably in a refugee camp — an old man too frail to endure another terrible winter in substandard conditions. He died in early 1863 and is buried nearby in an unmarked grave.

Recent efforts to revive this forgotten chief's legacy have been led by the Kansas Institute for African American and Native American Family History. The outdoor kiosk in LeRoy, dedicated in 2004, features a large historical plaque that tells the story of Opothle Yahola's "great escape" and the valiant service of the Indian Home Guard. After reading it, we couldn't help wondering why this courageous band had been treated so shabbily in Kansas.

☞ **Near here:** Humboldt sites, about 34 miles (see Index)

Pea Ridge National Military Park ⑫

★ *A Big Divide Top Site* ★

near Garfield, Arkansas (15930 East Highway 62)

Large battlefield and visitor center. Hours: Battlefield 6 a.m. to 9 p.m. daily from May to October, 6 to 6 November to April. Visitor Center is open 8 to 5 daily except Thanksgiving, Christmas, and New Year's Day. Admission: $5 per person. A 7-day pass for vehicles is $10, motorcycles $5. ⓖ: Visitor Center and some tour stops, notably East Lookout. Who runs it: National Park Service (nps.gov/peri). ☎ 479-451-8122.

 Our Take
Missouri's most important battlefield is in Arkansas, magnificently maintained and interpreted. A must-see.

General Earl Van Dorn had been sent west in the hopes of securing enough of Missouri to give the Confederates access to the Mississippi River. But his Army of the West was turned back near the state line at a strategic crossroads in Arkansas.

By March of 1862 the newly formed Union Army of the Southwest, under Samuel R. Curtis, had pushed the rebel army out of Missouri. Van Dorn was brought in to push back, but also to manage the relationship between generals Ben McCulloch and Sterling Price, who had stopped speaking to each other. The Confederates had a

The scenic East Lookout at Pea Ridge National Military Park.

numerical advantage at Pea Ridge, but the Union had a plethora of up-and-coming officers with names like Dodge, Asboth, Carr, and above all, Sheridan. Curtis would give them a chance to prove their mettle.

The confrontation took place March 7-8, 1862, in brutal conditions that forced soldiers to sleep on the frozen ground. The turning point came on the first day, when Union snipers killed McCulloch and his second-in-command. By the second day the Federals had achieved tactical superiority and in a classic show of force simply ran over their enemy, scattering rebels to the hills. Historian James M. McPherson, in his magisterial *Battle Cry of Freedom,* wrote that Pea Ridge for the rebel army was "as inglorious a rout in reverse as Bull Run," a reference to the earlier Civil War battle where the Confederates had forced Union troops to "skedaddle."

One of just 45 Civil War battlefields rated Class A for its strategic importance, Pea Ridge is also considered the most pristine site of its kind. The visitor center exhibits, updated in 2010, include a state-of-the-art multimedia retelling of each phase of the battle. Even the more traditional displays have clear, concise signage to maximize their interest.

Highlights of the battlefield's seven-mile, ten-stop auto tour are the East Lookout — an extraordinary vista — the restored Elkhorn Tavern that marked a turning point in the battle, and the open plain where it is possible to see the rout unfold, as Union soldiers charged in a mile-wide phalanx and the artillery pounded Confederates with hot lead. There are long hiking and horse trails and a decent cell phone audio tour.

Try to come in the late spring or fall, when the Ozarks put on a nature show with few rivals.

☛ **Battle casualties:** Union 1,384 of 10,500 (13 percent), Confederate 2,000 of 16,500 (12.5 percent).

Local Museum Spotlight

💬 Our Take
Not much Civil War-related at this museum, but it was one of our favorite "crowded closets."

Humboldt Historical Society Museum ❼
Humboldt, Kansas (2nd and Neosho). Hours: 1:30 to 4 weekends, June to October, or by appointment. **Free.** ♿: Mostly. Who runs it: Humboldt Historical Society (📞 620-473-5055).

Five, count 'em five buildings, including an 1867 stone house, barely seem sufficient to contain all the stuff collected by the friendly and enthusiastic volunteers who run the Humboldt museum. The Civil War display here is modest, but we include it in this chapter because the raid on Osceola led to the burning of this town (see Humboldt Civil War Tour, page 116) and because the route of Opothle Yahola's escape passed by here. Items at the museum include the bed where baseball legend Walter Johnson was born, military uniforms, horse-drawn hearses (adult and child sizes), a restored 1823 cannon, a Kansas license plate display, and a working old-fashioned windmill. But the highlight is Annex 5, containing hundreds of delightful scale-model horse-drawn wagons, buggies, and other conveyances made from wood by local hobbyist Lewis Howland, who clearly did not know when to stop.

And this is just one wall of Lewis Howland's creations inside Annex 5 at the Humboldt Historical Society Museum.

Driving Tours

Here are some ways to plan your historical and cultural journey through the Missouri-Kansas border region. You can easily customize your tour around one site or one town, or by wandering through the cross-references we've sprinkled throughout this guide. For more destination ideas, use the Orientation Map (page 248) and Index to look up individual cities and towns and learn what's there.

Tour 1: Circle of Presidents

For serious travelers and history buffs! Make The Big Divide part of a larger, five-state tour of national museums and historic sites for six U.S. presidents.

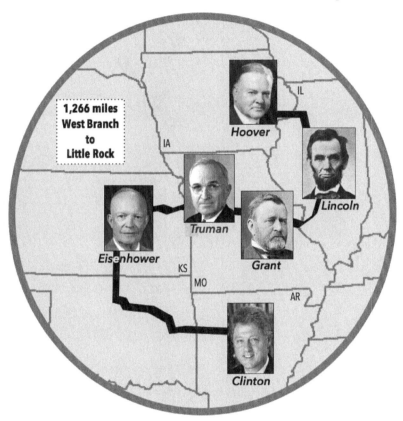

- Herbert Hoover Library & Museum, Herbert Hoover National Historic Site (West Branch, IA), president from 1929–1933
- Abraham Lincoln Presidential Library & Museum (Springfield, IL), 1861–65
- Ulysses S. Grant National Historic Site (St. Louis, MO), 1869–77
- Harry S. Truman Library & Museum, Harry S. Truman National Historic Site (Independence, MO; see page 205), 1945–53
- Dwight D. Eisenhower Presidential Library & Museum (Abilene, KS), 1953–61
- William J. Clinton Presidential Center (Little Rock, AR), 1993–2001

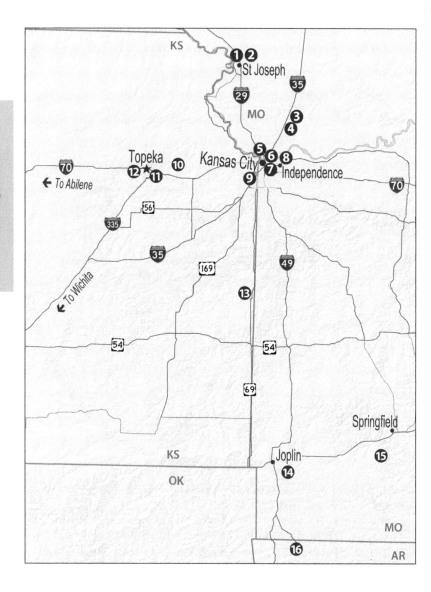

Tour 2: Big Divide Top Sites

275 miles roundtrip (sites 1–12) or 700 miles (all sites)

When you only have time for the best. This driving tour spotlights the most authentic and best interpreted historic and cultural places in the Missouri-Kansas border region.

1. Glore Psychiatric Museum, St. Joseph, MO (page 219)

2. Patee House Museum, St. Joseph, MO (page 61)

3. Watkins Woolen Mill State Historic Site, Lawson, MO (page 185)

4. Jesse James Farm and Museum, Kearney, MO (page 175)

5. Nelson-Atkins Museum of Art, Kansas City, MO (page 44)

6. Arabia Steamboat Museum, Kansas City, MO (page 59)

7. National World War I Museum at Liberty Memorial, Kansas City, MO (page 210)

8. Harry S. Truman Presidential Library and Museum, Independence, MO (page 205)

9. Shawnee Indian Mission State Historic Site, Fairway, KS (page 39)

10. Constitution Hall State Historic Site, Lecompton, KS (page 87)

11. Brown v. Board of Education National Historic Site, Topeka, KS (page 211)

12. Kansas Museum of History, Topeka (page 78)

13. Mine Creek Battlefield State Historic Site, Pleasanton, KS (page 171)

14. George Washington Carver National Monument, Diamond, MO (page 191)

15. Wilson's Creek National Battlefield, Republic, MO (page 111)

16. Pea Ridge National Military Park, Garfield, AR (page 119)

Tour 3: African American Heritage

300 miles roundtrip (sites 1-11) or 330 miles (sites 4-5 and 10-13) or 700 miles (all)
From the first black fighting regiment to the end of school segregation,
African American history was made here. Consider extending your trip to
Nicodemus National Historic Site in western Kansas.

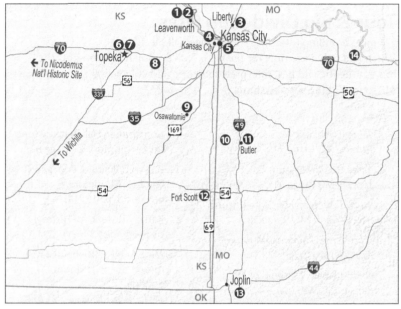

1. Buffalo Soldier Monument/
   Ft. Sully, Fort Leavenworth,
   KS (page 173)

2. Richard Allen Cultural Center,
   Leavenworth, KS (page 184)

3. Freedom Fountain, Liberty,
   MO (page 185)

4. Quindaro Overlook, Kansas
   City, KS (page 94)

5. Negro Leagues Baseball Museum/
   American Jazz Museum,
   Kansas City, MO (page 213)

6. Brown v. Board of Education,
   Topeka, KS (page 211)

7. Kansas State Capitol (John Brown
   mural), Topeka (page 86)

8. John Brown Museum,
   Osawatomie, KS (page 89)

9. Wakarusa River Valley
   Heritage Museum, near
   Lawrence, KS (page 95)

10. Battle of Island Mound
    State Historic Site, near
    Butler, MO (page 146)

11. First Kansas Colored Infantry
    Monument and Bates County
    Museum, Butler, MO (page 147)

12. Gordon Parks sites in Fort
    Scott, KS (page 193)

13. George Washington
    Carver Nat'l Monument,
    Diamond, MO (page 191)

14. Brown Lodge at Historic
    Arrow Rock, MO (page 152)

Tour 4: Battlefields and Cemeteries

680 miles roundtrip

Military clashes along the border lasted from May 1856 (historic Black Jack) to October 1864 (Second Newtonia).

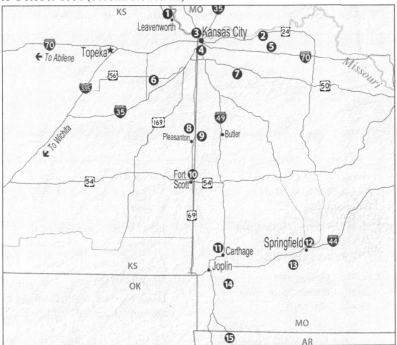

1. Fort Leavenworth Nat'l Cemetery, KS (page 173)

2. Battle of Lexington, MO (page 113)

3. Battle of Westport, Kansas City, MO (page 169)

4. Union Cemetery, Kansas City, MO (page 172)

5. Confederate Memorial, Higginsville, MO (page 174)

6. Black Jack Battlefield, near Baldwin City, KS (page 91)

7. Lone Jack Civil War Museum, Lone Jack, MO (page 143)

8. Mine Creek Battlefield, Pleasanton, KS (page 171)

9. Battle of Island Mound, near Butler, MO (page 146)

10. Fort Scott Nat'l Cemetery, KS (page 173)

11. Battle of Carthage, MO (page 109)

12. Springfield National Cemetery, MO (page 113)

13. Wilson's Creek National Battlefield, Republic, MO (page 111)

14. Battles of Newtonia, MO (page 144)

15. Pea Ridge National Military Park, Garfield, AR (page 119)

Driving Tours

Tour 5: Art Titans

Benton sites 30 miles, Bingham sites 225 miles, Curry sites 250 miles (roundtrips from Kansas City, MO)

Thomas Hart Benton, George Caleb Bingham, and John Steuart Curry defined and celebrated this region's history through their paintings.

1. Arrow Rock State Historic Site, Arrow Rock, MO, Bingham (page 152)

2. Harry S. Truman Presidential Museum, Independence, MO, Benton (page 205)

3. Bingham-Waggoner Estate, Independence, MO, Bingham (page 152)

4. Thomas Hart Benton State Historic Site, Kansas City, MO (page 206)

5. Nelson-Atkins Museum of Art, Kansas City, MO, Benton/Bingham (page 44)

6. John Steuart Curry Boyhood Home, Oskaloosa, KS (page 86)

7. Kansas State Capitol, Topeka, Curry (page 86)

8. Beach Museum of Art, Manhattan, KS, Curry (page 86)

Rozzelle Court at Nelson-Atkins Museum of Art.

Tour 6: Historic Homes

210 miles roundtrip (sites 2–11), 380 miles (all sites)

Nothing here but beautifully restored, historically important homes. Amelia Earhart Birthplace site is self-guided; all the others offer guided tours.

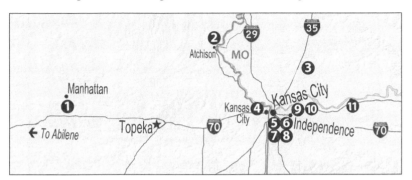

1. Goodnow House, Manhattan, KS (page 190)

2. Amelia Earhart Birthplace, Atchison, KS (page 218)

3. Watkins House at Watkins Woolen Mill, Lawson, MO (page 185)

4. Grinter Place, Kansas City, KS (page 52)

5. Thomas Hart Benton Home, Kansas City, MO (page 206)

6. Harris-Kearney House, Kansas City, MO (page 57)

7. John Wornall House Museum, Kansas City, MO (page 170)

8. Alexander Majors House, Kansas City, MO (page 62)

9. Bingham-Waggoner Estate, Independence, MO (page 152)

10. Harry S. Truman Home and Noland Home, Independence, MO (page 207)

11. Anderson House at the Battle of Lexington, MO (page 113)

Amelia Earhart Birthplace in Atchison, Kansas.

Driving Tours

Tour 7: Indian Country

250 miles roundtrip (sites 1–9), 575 miles (all sites)

Kansas was home to many emigrant tribes from 1830 to 1854 (see page 28). The Osages dominated the region from 1700 to 1800.

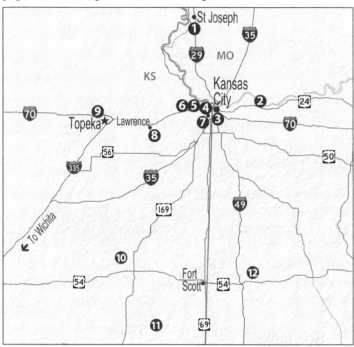

1. St. Joseph Museums, St. Joseph, MO (page 43)

2. Fort Osage, Sibley, MO (page 32)

3. Nelson-Atkins Museum of Art, Kansas City, MO (page 44)

4. Huron Indian Cemetery, Kansas City, KS (page 37)

5. Kaw Point, Kansas City, KS (page 30)

6. Wyandotte County Museum, Bonner Springs, KS (page 36)

7. Shawnee Indian Mission, Fairway, KS (page 39)

8. Haskell Cultural Center, Lawrence, KS (page 215)

9. Kansas Museum of History, Topeka (page 78)

10. Opothle Yahola Memorial, LeRoy, KS (page 117)

11. Osage Mission, St. Paul, KS (page 45)

12. Osage Village, near Walker, MO (page 33)

Tour 8: Scenic Highway 52

48 miles one-way

Eight diverse sites, including two historic battlefields, on a short cross-state drive about an hour south of Kansas City. (Note: Kansas 52 shares US-69 between Pleasanton and Trading Post.)

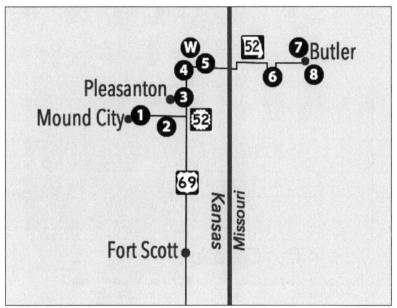

1. Mound City Historical Park (page 197) and Soldiers' Lot, Mound City, KS (page 172)

2. Mine Creek Battlefield, Pleasanton, KS (page 171)

3. Linn County Historical Museum, Pleasanton, KS (page 177)

4. Trading Post Museum, Pleasanton, KS (page 65)

5. Marais des Cygnes Massacre Site, near Pleasanton, KS (page 93)

6. Battle of Island Mound, near Butler, MO (page 146)

7. Bates County Museum, Butler, MO (page 160)

8. First Kansas Colored Volunteer Infantry Monument, Butler, MO (page 147)

W. Marais des Cygnes State Wildlife Area and Marais des Cygnes National Wildlife Refuge

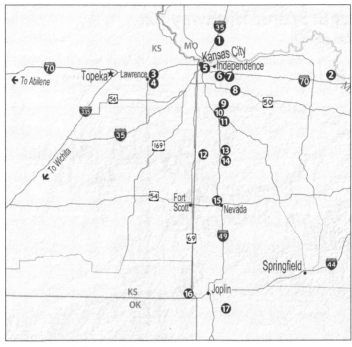

Sites in This Chapter

1. Clay County Museum, Liberty, MO
2. Historic Arrow Rock, MO
3. Lawrence Visitor Center, Lawrence, KS
4. Watkins Community Museum of History, Lawrence, KS
5. Union Prison Collapse, Kansas City, MO
6. 1859 Jail, Independence, MO
7. Bingham-Waggoner Estate, Independence, MO
8. Lone Jack Civil War Museum, Lone Jack, MO
9. Pleasant Hill Post Office, Pleasant Hill, MO
10. Burnt District Museum, Harrisonville, MO
11. Burnt District Monument, Harrisonville, MO
12. Battle of Island Mound State Historic Site, MO
13. Bates County Museum, Butler, MO
14. First Kansas Colored Volunteer Monument, Butler, MO
15. Bushwhacker Museum and Jail, Nevada, MO
16. Baxter Springs Heritage Center, Baxter Springs, KS
17. First Battle of Newtonia, MO

Tip: The Index lists all sites in every town.

Detail from William Philyaw's diorama of the burning of Lawrence at the Lone Jack Civil War Museum (page 143).

∽✸✸ 6 ∽✸✸

Guerrilla War

With the threat of a Confederate Army invasion of Missouri eliminated, guerrilla bands emerged as the chief threat to the Union — not only to Federal garrisons but to any civilian suspected of being a Northern sympathizer. There were also pro-Union Jayhawkers, including the ruthless "Red Legs" (for their distinctive hosiery), who sacked farms or villages thought to be aiding Confederate guerrillas — or simply having pro-Southern views. In this way thousands of households and farms were robbed and burned during the war, its occupants killed or forced to flee. Guerrilla violence was a problem in all the border states during the Civil War, but the lingering bitterness from the Bleeding Kansas period, the growing hostility toward Union troops occupying Missouri, and the ever-porous boundary with Kansas made for an explosive combination. Historians consider the fighting here from 1862 to 1864 to be the worst guerrilla warfare in U.S. history.

Even though the Union Army beefed up its presence in Missouri to 50,000 troops, and declared martial law through the border region in February 1862, it could not stop the attacks by pro-Southern guerrillas, often called Bushwhackers (**Bushwhacker Museum and Jail,** page 141). Making matters worse, many Missourians believed that Union troops were turning a blind eye to attacks by Jayhawkers and even taking part in the looting of homes. These civilians grew to despise their Federal occupiers and began actively supporting the guerrillas. This led to even more repressive measures by the Union Army — a vicious cycle that made the region increasingly unstable.

In August 1862, a small band of Confederates rode up from Arkansas to Jackson County, Missouri, and made contact with guerrillas led by a former schoolteacher from Ohio named William Clarke Quantrill. The forces they scared up surprised a Union garrison at Independence and sent hundreds of terrified Federals fleeing all the way to Kansas City. Word of the rout spread quickly, lifting the spirits of everyone who had given up hope after the defeat at Pea Ridge.

Rebel commanders soon sent up 1,500 reinforcements from Arkansas and deputized Quantrill's men as Partisan Rangers. This unit — created expressly for guerrilla forces — scored a resounding victory in five hours of intense fighting at the **Battle of Lone Jack** (page 143).

Although Quantrill was elsewhere when hostilities broke out at Lone Jack, he would make his presence known throughout the fall. In September his raiders crossed into Kansas and sacked Olathe, killing at least seventeen and making off with wagons of plunder. There would be Quantrill sightings in Cass County and Lafayette County, Missouri; Shawneetown, Kansas; and along the Santa Fe Trail. Meanwhile, Southern forces entered southwest Missouri and inflicted heavy casualties on a Union artillery division in Newtonia. The **First Battle of Newtonia** (page 144) was a rare Civil War battle in that Native American regiments fought on *both* sides.

These military losses, along with the terror inflicted by Quantrill's raiders, revealed how tenuous the Union's grip on Missouri actually was beyond Federal garrisons and the major rivers it controlled. The events of 1862 also showed that rebel commanders could work effectively with Bushwhackers to intimidate much larger Union forces.

Guerrillas led by former schoolteacher William Clarke Quantrill sent terrified Federals fleeing all the way to Kansas City.

Over in Kansas, Jim Lane had begun drilling black men in militia units with the idea of sending them to deal with the guerrilla threat. It was an historic experiment that would soon pay tremendous dividends for the Union Army. For years slaves had been escaping to the North, sometimes using the safe houses of the Underground Railroad. But now, thanks to the Civil War, the path to liberation was as close as the nearest picket of Federal troops. Thousands of African Americans liberated themselves by running to Union lines,

Thomas Nast, the famed illustrator for *Harper's Weekly*, drew the Civil War with a Northern flavor. This woodcut, "Rebel Guerrilla Raid in a Western Town," appeared in the September 27, 1862 issue. Though the scene is a composite from various newspaper reports, the most likely target of Nast's propaganda was William Clarke Quantrill, whose exploits had started to appear in the national press. Notice the rough treatment of women and the raider shooting a little dog for fun.

then worked for the Army as manual laborers, laundresses, cooks, teamsters, and eventually as soldiers.

This emancipation of Missouri slaves left their former masters stunned and outraged. Many had assumed that because they supported the Union, they would be allowed to keep their slaves after the war. Others felt their worst fears had been confirmed. This was turning into a war to free the slaves and destroy the Southern way of life. Some Missourians blamed Jayhawkers like Charles "Doc" Jennison for "stealing" their slaves, as if it might not occur to people in bondage to liberate themselves. As historian Diane Mutti Burke put it, "Enslaved Missourians capitalized on the presence of the

Union military and the political divisions among the white population and left their owners by the thousands."

If Missouri slaveholders were whipsawed by the sudden turn of events, so were Lincoln's generals in Washington. They spent much of 1862 delaying the mustering of African Americans into Federal battalions. That is how it came to be that the first black soldiers to die in defense of the Union actually belonged to a state militia unit organized by a Jayhawker. Thanks to the acclaimed film *Glory*, it has been long assumed that the 54th Massachusetts was the first regiment of black troops to fight and die in the Civil War. In fact, it was the First Kansas Colored Volunteer Infantry who entered the field of combat first, holding off a superior force of Confederate guerrillas on a piece of Missouri prairie known as Island Mound on October 29, 1862.

For years the only monument to this historic achievement was a small marker stone in the Fort Scott National Cemetery (page 40). But recently the town of Butler, Missouri, has embraced these African American fighters, led by local historian Chris Tabor and the Amen Society, founded by the Rev. Larry Coleman. The **First Kansas Colored Volunteer Infantry Monument** (page 147) was dedicated in 2008, and the State of Missouri followed in 2012 with the **Battle of Island Mound State Historic Site** (page 146), west of town. During the Civil War, Butler was so firmly "secesh" that Lane's Brigade ransacked the town in 1861, and in 1863 the surrounding area would be cleared out and burned to the ground by Federals. Yet today Butler celebrates a black infantry regiment raised by James H. Lane. He would be astounded.

The guerrilla attacks on Federal forces in Missouri persisted into the summer of 1863. Increasingly, General Thomas Ewing, the Army's commander along the border, saw no reason to distinguish between Bushwhackers and the civilian population that supported them.

His troops, many of them from anti-slavery states, looked with disdain on the Missourians. "The inhabitants here are most all very ignorant and consequently Secesh," a soldier from Maine wrote home. The feeling was mutual. No hearts or minds were won as Federal troops aggressively patrolled the border, harassing residents while doing little to stop the brutality of the "Red Legs" from Kansas.

But Ewing had more than a public relations problem. He had a family problem on his hands — namely the wives, mothers, and sisters of guerrillas. Not only were these strong-minded women running the households while the men were away,

Pro-Union guerrillas like Charles "Doc" Jennison (shown kidnapping a woman in this Confederate sketch) were as feared and reviled as guerrillas who supported the rebellion.

but Ewing realized they were secretly supplying their relatives with food and forage, shelter, horses, guns, and intelligence about Union troop movements. As occupiers are wont to do, Ewing responded to this threat by rounding up suspects and throwing them in detention.

The more fortunate women were imprisoned in a well-built structure like the **1859 Jail** in Independence (page 148), which later provided a comfortable place for Frank James to await trial after the war. One unfortunate group, however, was herded into a dank tavern in Kansas City that had been once been a studio for the artist **George Caleb Bingham** (see page 150) and was later commandeered as a Union prison. On August 13, 1863, the building collapsed, killing "Bloody Bill" Anderson's 14-year-old sister and three other women related to Quantrill gang members.

Whether to avenge these deaths, or because it just seemed like the time to strike, Quantrill and Anderson led 400 men into the abolitionist town of Lawrence, Kansas, on the morning of August 21 and laid waste to it.

There has been no permanent exhibit on Quantrill's Lawrence raid and its aftermath — the issuing of General Order No. 11 on the Missouri side four days later. For that matter, given Quantrill's continued cultural resonance, it is surprising that no historic site besides the tiny **Burnt District Museum** (page 156) has been devoted to the events of August 1863. But this situation is changing. In August 2013, on the 150th anniversary of the raid, Lawrence's **Watkins Community Museum of History** (page 154) will open a newly-renovated gallery that puts Quantrill and his day of infamy front and center.

A flower-bedecked sign in downtown Kansas City marks the site of the Union Prison Collapse (page 148).

Ewing, the Union commander, had been pondering what to do with the civilian insurgency. On August 18, after the prison collapse but before the Lawrence massacre, Ewing issued General Order No. 10, which would have evicted anyone found to be assisting the rebellion along the District of the Border (running about 100 miles south of the Missouri River). Just one week later, after Lawrence, he went even further, issuing General Order No. 11 — probably the most devastating and least well-understood military action of the Trans-Mississippi Civil War. Some 20,000 residents of Jackson, Cass, Bates, and Vernon counties were ordered to leave the area immediately. Jayhawkers were enlisted to burn the homes and fields left behind, to prevent guerrillas from using them for shelter and forage.

And thus the District of the Border took on a new name — the Burnt District. The trauma of the mass evacuation, and perhaps a little guilt over his relationship to the structure that had collapsed, led Bingham to pick up his brush and create his last major painting, a work he titled *Martial Law* but everyone else called *Order No. 11* (page 150). The Burnt District would later inspire memorial art by Tom Lea in a mural at the **Pleasant Hill Post Office** (page 158) and, just recently, the striking **Burnt District Memorial** (page 156).

In the fall of 1863, as Quantrill and his men departed for winter quarters in Texas — having lost the tree foliage they relied on for cover — they engaged the Second Kansas Colored Regiment at Fort Blair in Baxter Springs, Kansas. Though unable to take the fort, Quantrill's attention was diverted to a wagon train crossing the prairie to the north. It turned out to be a Federal supply train of men and boys. The slaughter that ensued is well documented at the **Baxter Springs Heritage Center and Museum** (page 158).

Bushwhacker Museum and Jail ⑮

Nevada, Missouri (212 West Walnut, in the lower level of the Finis M. Moss Building; the jail is two blocks away)

Museum and historic jail. Hours: 10 to 4 Wednesday thru Saturday, May to October. Admission: $5 adults, $2 ages 12-17, $1 under 12. &: Yes for museum (using elevator) and jail (first floor only). Who runs it: Vernon County Historical Society. ✆ 417-667-9602.

 Our Take

Interesting storehouse of Bushwhacker culture explains the depth of support for Confederate guerrillas.

This well-kept and professionally-run little museum in the "Bushwhacker capital" of Nevada documents the turmoil that engulfed southwest Missouri during the Civil War. Nevada — named for the Wild West town of Nevada City but pronounced neh-VAY-dah — had no interest in the Union cause. Indeed, Vernon County sent more soldiers to fight for the Confederacy than any other Missouri county. Many remain proud of that fact.

In the museum, the orientation film helps explain the forces at work locally during the Civil War, the burning of the area, and the town's resurrection afterward. You also learn about two historic enterprises located a few blocks from the museum — the W.F. Norman Co., which still produces decorative tiles and tin shingles from its 100-year-old catalog of designs; and Cottey College, a unique women's school owned and operated by the P.E.O. Sisterhood, making it the only fully woman-owned college in the country.

But you didn't come for that. You came to see authentic Confederate flags, Bowie knives, guns, swords, uniforms, and period apparel and to read about the glory days of Bushwhacking. Fear not — the museum has you covered, and it continues to add to its collection. There is even an exhibit on a "lady Bushwhacker," Eliza Gabbert, who was a spy, scout, and comrade of the male Bushwhackers in the county. Small wonder the Union Army had to park thousands of its men along the Missouri border with no battles to fight, instead of sending them back East where they were urgently needed.

During the war every town in Vernon County was put to the torch but one. Federal troops burned Nevada on May 26, 1863, leaving only a few buildings, including the city jail. Now known as the Bushwhacker Jail, a guided tour of the two-story facility is included with your museum admission. The museum is also a repository for artifacts from nearby Osage Village (page 33).

☛ **Local color:** Every June for almost 50 years, Nevadans have celebrated **Bushwhacker Days,** a four-day carnival with music, cookouts, and historical reenactments.

☛ **Near here:** A historical marker at the jail site commemorates the **Battle of Dry Wood Creek**, when Sterling Price's Missouri State Guard defeated Jim Lane's brigade in 1861, capturing their mules — hence the other name for the skirmish, the Battle of the Mules.

Lone Jack Civil War Museum ❽

Lone Jack, Missouri (301 South Bynum Road, just off Highway 50)

Museum with historic cemetery. Hours: 10 to 4 Wednesdays through Saturdays and 1 to 4 Sundays March to October, open weekend hours the rest of the year. Admission: $3 for ages 13+ and $1 for ages 6-12. ♿: Yes. Who runs it: Lone Jack Historical Society (historiclonejack.org). ☎ 816-805-1815.

 Our Take

Excellent introduction to the Civil War in western Missouri.

One of Harry Truman's fondest childhood memories was going with his father to the annual Democratic picnic, held in eastern Jackson County on the site of the Battle of Lone Jack. After his presidency Truman helped raise money to build this distinctive round museum of native stone that commemorates the victory by Confederates and pro-Southern guerrillas. Thanks to the dedicated volunteers who maintain it, the Lone Jack museum has added exhibits that make it a much better introduction to the Civil War on the western Missouri front than its small size would indicate. (Good website, too.)

Harry Truman helped raise money for the Lone Jack Civil War Museum.

A small Confederate force bolstered by a guerrilla army attacked Independence on August 11, 1862. That led to this confrontation at Lone Jack in eastern Jackson County five days later. Militia under the command of Union Maj. Emory Foster were supposed to be reinforced by an infantry unit of Iowa volunteers. But the Iowans arrived too late, leaving Foster's men to fend off a force four times their size. Foster and nearly all of his officers were wounded, some mortally, in five hours of intense fighting. Within days Jackson County came under Federal occupation again. But these victories were not long forgotten, and their memory was kept alive for decades at the Democratic picnic in Lone Jack.

For the museum's opening in 1963, artist William Philyaw created the four extraordinary dioramas that dazzle visitors to this day (see photo, page 133). Lone Jack also has artifacts from the fighting and a new timeline of the major battles of Missouri's Civil War. The cemetery behind the museum holds the remains of both Union and Confederate soldiers in mass graves. Each Memorial Day, the battlefield is illuminated with candles from dusk to dark.

☛ **Battle casualties:** Casualty numbers for this and other battles in Missouri are hard to estimate, since many of the fighters lived nearby and were carried off by family members when they fell. Approximate troop strength at Lone Jack was 3,000 Confederates and 800 Federals. It is said only half of the latter escaped.

The Battles of Newtonia ⑰
Newtonia, Missouri (Matthew Ritchey Mansion, 520 Mill Street)

Historic home with exhibits and interpretive signage outside. Open by appointment only. **Free.** ♿: Call. Who runs it: Newtonia Battlefields Protection Association, which offers free tours. Call Tom at 417-437-5974.

 Our Take
Don't overlook this site, noted for its two battles and opposing Indian regiments. Call ahead for a guided tour.

The best-kept secret among Civil War buffs in these parts is Newtonia, site of two Confederate victories in 1862 and 1864. The Matthew H. Ritchey Home features exhibits, battle artifacts, and a striking mural by painter Dale Long. It's worth a guided tour — which is the only way to access this developing site. Come early and read the interpretive signage under the canopy while you wait for your guide.

The First Battle of Newtonia came about after large numbers of Confederates began congregating here, obtaining access to nearby military roads, flour mills, and lead mines for bullets. Federals arrived on September 30, 1862, to repel the invaders.

Both sides had Indian regiments deployed. The Third Indian Home Guard fought alongside the Federals (for more on the Indian Home Guard, see Opothle Yahola Memorial, page 117). Back and forth the battle raged for twelve hours. As darkness fell, Union forces

Two "signs" of Newtonia's growing importance in Civil War history were recently installed by the State of Missouri — one for each battle fought there.

began a retreat with trailing cannon fire, only to be shellacked by accurate return fire. Once again, though, the rebels could not hold their win at Newtonia.

☞ **Battle casualties:** Union 245 of 1,500 (16 percent), Confederates 100 out of unknown army size

The Second Battle of Newtonia took place two years later, on October 28, 1864, as Confederate general Sterling Price was in full retreat following his failed raid of Missouri. Union forces caught up to Price's army as it approached the Arkansas state line. As at Westport and Mine Creek, General Jo Shelby rode to the rescue, ordering his cavalrymen to dismount and fire on the advancing Federals. Union forces suffered nearly three times as many casualties here as they had a few days earlier at the Battle of Mine Creek (page 171).

☞ **Battle casualties:** Union 400, Confederates 250

Battle of Island Mound State Historic Site ⑫

Bates County, Missouri (7 miles west of Butler)

Historic park. Open dawn to dusk. **Free.** ♿: Trail is gravel, fairly level, with a gentle rise. Who runs it: Missouri State Parks. ℂ 417-276-4259.

 Our Take

Missouri's newest state park gives the First Kansas Colored's place in history its due.

With this historic site, the State of Missouri has finally given official recognition to the role of these first African-American soldiers to fight — and die — in defense of the Union.

The First Kansas Colored Volunteer Infantry were charged with clearing out pro-Southern guerrillas who had gathered in Bates County. They were met by a force twice their size — as many as 500 Bushwhackers. What the Kansas infantry had going for them were superior weaponry and a determination to stand their ground. You may hear it said that rebel soldiers "gave no quarter" to their black counterparts. That's a nice way of saying that any wounded or captured soldiers from the Colored regiment were executed on the spot. That is what would happen to members of the First Kansas at battles in Sherwood, Missouri, and Poison Spring, Arkansas.

The black men in blue weren't just fighting for their lives but for respect and acceptance — and that would be hard to come by, even from their fellow soldiers. As Gen. Don Scott, a champion of Island Mound (in the photo he's the one in a Buffalo Soldier hat), likes to point out, the resolve of black soldiers would be questioned every time the U.S. went to war until Harry Truman finally integrated the armed forces in 1948.

The brand-new Island Mound park consists of interpretive signage, an easy half-mile walking trail around a pleasant 40-acre patch of prairie, and a picnic shelter. The land that was acquired is where nearly 250 black soldiers and officers and one Indian soldier bivouacked for three days. They commandeered the farm of a jailed Bushwhacker, added some fence rails as reinforcements, and dubbed it "Fort Africa." South of here, they would suffer light casualties, counter a brush fire lit by the enemy with their own backfire, chase off the rebels, and make national news.

Ribbon-cutting for Island Mound State Historic Site near Butler, Missouri, October 27, 2012.

☛ **Picnic alert:** Park managers clearly want the Battle of Island Mound park to be a place for family reunions and other gatherings. The covered picnic shelter includes an enormous grill.

☛ **Near here:** Besides the two sites listed below, five other stops are a short drive away along scenic Highway 52 (see page 131).

First Kansas Colored Volunteer Infantry Monument ⑭

Butler, Missouri (on the courthouse square, 7 West Ohio Street)

Statue. ♿: Yes. Erected by Amen Society and Butler citizens.

 Our Take

Fine statue celebrates history-making soldiers.

In 2008 local and state officials gathered for the unveiling of this statue that pays tribute to the country's first black regiment to see combat in the Civil War. Besides the usual civic pride that accompanies discovery of a historic "first," this tribute to the First Kansas Colored was striking for taking place in a onetime Confederate stronghold. Then again, Butler was essentially a rebooted town after the Civil War. Having been emptied out by

General Order No. 11, it was repopulated by migrants who had not experienced the hardships of life on the border in the Civil War, nor harbored any resentments against the Union.

The sculptor of this monument, Joel Randall, specializes in classical realist representations. His soldier projects both the manly ideals of the ancient warriors and the rugged authenticity of a Mathew Brady photograph.

Union Prison Collapse ❺

Kansas City, Missouri (at Truman and Grand, across from Sprint Center on I–670 viaduct)

Historical marker. ♿: Yes. Erected by Native Sons and Daughters of KC.

 Our Take

Worth stopping at this sign when in downtown Kansas City.

There are hundreds of historical markers on both sides of The Big Divide. We highlight this one because of its relevance to our story. Also, as you can see from the picture on page 140, it is beautifully tended and convenient to downtown Kansas City, which you may be visiting anyway. (It is adjacent to a popular entertainment district built around the Sprint Center.)

When an overcrowded jail collapsed near this site in 1863, four women died, including the 14-year-old sister of "Bloody Bill" Anderson. The Quantrill-Anderson massacre at Lawrence was fueled by the prison collapse, and the raid in turn hastened the deportation of Missourians here and in three other counties along the border. There were, in fact, many causes and effects surrounding these events, more than one historical marker can include. The deaths of four young women in Kansas City were but part of a much larger chain of tragedies along the border in 1863.

1859 Jail, Marshal's Home and Museum ❻

Independence, Missouri (217 North Main Street on the town square)

Historic jail with museum exhibits. Hours: 10 to 4 Monday thru Saturday and 1 to 4 Sunday, April to October only. Admission: $6 adults, $5 seniors,

$3 youth 5-15. ♿: Call. Who runs it: Jackson County Historical Society (jchs.org). ☏ 816-252-1892.

🗨 Our Take
A cut above other historic jails. Displays add interest.

This two-story, Federal-style brick structure houses twelve limestone jail cells and, as was common at the time, the residence of the marshal. This was a Union jail during the Civil War, except for a brief time in 1862 after Partisan Rangers led by William Quantrill liberated it following the First Battle of Independence. Otherwise, it was often full to overflowing during the war, with local citizens who had been arrested on suspicion of sabotage or aiding the rebels. When this jail was full, officials commissioned other buildings to serve as holding cells, including the site of the infamous Union Prison Collapse (see above).

Frank James was treated as a celebrity, eating dinner with the jail's marshal and attending the opera.

The 1859 Jail's most famous prisoner was Frank James, Jesse's brother. When he was jailed here awaiting trial he was treated as a celebrity, eating dinner with the marshal and going to Independence Square to attend the opera.

When you enter the museum you will be in what used to be the marshal's dining room, now the gift shop. You're given a brochure for a self-guided tour. Most of the rooms are self-explanatory or have adequate signage. A 1905 addition to the jail has relics, photos, and exhibits from Jackson County's Civil War years.

George Caleb Bingham
and 'Order No. 11'

Martial Law by George Caleb Bingham (1811–1879), popularly known as *Order No. 11*, has had a cultural impact matched by few pieces of American art. No book, no speech or sculpture, has done more than Bingham's last major work to preserve the memory of General Thomas Ewing's General Order No. 11 and its devastating effect on people in western Missouri during the Civil War. *Order No. 11* today adorns virtually every historic house and museum in the Burnt District of western Missouri.

Self-Portrait of the Artist (1834-35) by George Caleb Bingham.

Raised on the edge of the frontier in Franklin and Arrow Rock, Missouri, Bingham taught himself portraiture and by age 19 was making a living at it, earning $20 at a time on commissions from as far away as St. Louis. He spent much of the 1840s and 1850s on the East Coast, developing a national reputation. His portrait of John Quincy Adams hangs in the National Gallery in Washington, D.C. At the Nelson-Atkins Museum (page 44), Dr. Benoist Troost, an early builder of Kansas City, holds a book in an 1859 posthumous portrait to convey his learnedness. Later Bingham turned to painting scenes of the provincial people he grew up around. These "genre paintings" would eventually confirm his status as one of the 19th century's masters.

Bingham was an unusual artist in that he loved politics and was eager to be in the thick of it. He served as a state assemblyman in 1848, Missouri state treasurer during the Civil War, and Kansas City police commissioner in 1874. He once wrote an influential friend, "I forget that I am a painter and not a politician," but his superb political genre paintings showed he could have it both ways (see, for example, *Country Politician* on page 153). Only when he painted *Order No. 11* toward the end of his life did the mixture of politics and painting turn volatile. That, as well as its melodramatic content, are why this painting failed to draw the critical acclaim Bingham felt it deserved.

Detail from an engraving of *Order No. 11* by George Caleb Bingham.

Legend has it that he painted *Order No. 11* in order to destroy the political career of Ewing, whose edict brought about the suffering depicted on the canvas. There is only one shred of evidence for this theory, however, supplied by a newspaper reporter in 1877, long after the fact. Bingham certainly despised Ewing for his cruelty, but one could just as well argue that the painter was driven by feelings of guilt for letting the Union Army turn his studio in Kansas City into a prison in July 1863. It collapsed the following month, part of a chain of events that led up to Ewing's order (see Union Prison Collapse, page 148).

Art historians generally discount the political theory in favor of an artistic one: Like John Steuart Curry with John Brown, Bingham had found a subject worthy of a grand historical painting to cement his legacy. He spent years painting it — twice — and had an engraving made so he could issue prints and widen its circulation. To his dismay, though, *Order No. 11* was attacked by critics in Missouri and Kansas, who treated it as a pro-Southern tract. Like

Curry's *Tragic Prelude*, something about *Order No. 11* touched a nerve close to home and revealed once more the bitter feelings that the Civil War had stirred up. Bingham, a staunch Unionist during the war, spent the last years of his life defending his work.

In the 1930s public galleries like the Metropolitan Museum of Art in New York began to acquire his works. Painters like Thomas Hart Benton (see page 206), Curry (page 84), and Grant Wood sparked interest in mid-American art, also to Bingham's benefit. With the artist's bicentennial in 2011, *Order No. 11* seems to be getting a fresh reappraisal and Bingham is at last getting credit for trying to wrap his arms around the explosive drama that was western Missouri in the Civil War.

George Caleb Bingham Sites We Like

Bingham-Waggoner Estate ❼
Independence, Missouri (313 West Pacific Avenue)

Historic home. Hours: 10 to 4 Monday thru Saturday, noon to 4 Sunday, March to October, plus holiday season. Admission: $6 adults, $5 seniors, $3 students. ♿: Call. Privately operated (bwestate.org). ✆ 816-461-3491.

For five years this home was owned by the Bingham family, and it was here that *Order No. 11* was painted. Bingham also ran for Congress while living here. Eventually the home passed to the Waggoners, who made their fortune in milling, operating their plant right across the street from the mansion. The house is a Victorian showpiece, open April to October and during the holidays for tours. It's located across from the National Frontier Trails Museum (page 55).

Historic Arrow Rock ❷
Arrow Rock, Missouri (17 miles NW of Boonville on Highway 41)

Restored 1830s village and State Historic Site with visitor center. Hours: Visitor Center open 10 to 4 daily, closing one hour later in summer. **Free.** Trams operate daily during summer and weekends in off-season; rides $5 for adults, $3.50 for children. ♿: Yes for Visitor Center and some sites in town. Who runs it: Village is privately owned; Historic Site is a Missouri State Park (mostateparks.com). ✆ 660-837-3330.

This one-of-a-kind village has fewer than 60 souls living in it

Detail from *Country Politician*, one of the acclaimed "genre paintings" Bingham took from political life of his native Missouri.

and takes in 150,000 visitors a year. That's because the whole town is a National Historic Landmark with a support group devoted wholeheartedly to its preservation. In-season tram rides take you to sites around town, including the 1837 house where Bingham lived as a young man. Arrow Rock has Missouri's oldest repertory theater, a popular lecture series, and a restaurant that has operated continuously since 1834. Two historic buildings were recently converted into professionally interpreted museums. The painstakingly restored Brown Lodge features the permanent exhibit "Reflections of African-American Arrow Rock, 1865-1960." Both museums are free, self-service, and generally open all day long, all year round.

Nelson-Atkins Museum of Art
see review on page 44

Bingham's "genre paintings," featuring riverboatmen, frontier settlers, country politicians, and other colorful characters he knew from rural Missouri, are widely considered to be American masterworks. The Nelson, one of our Big Divide Top Sites (see page 44), has more than two dozen Binghams in its collection as well a large number of the artist's sketches and studies. Besides the Nelson, the State Historical Society of Missouri in Columbia (page 228) has numerous Binghams in its collection.

Watkins Community Museum of History ❹

Lawrence, Kansas (1047 Massachusetts)

County museum in historic building. Hours: 10 to 4 Tuesday thru Saturday, open until 8 p.m. Thursday from April-November. **Free.** ♿: Yes (enter on 11th Street for elevator). Who runs it: Douglas County Historical Society (watkinsmuseum.org). ✆ 785-841-4109.

Our Take

Quantrill will soon get his due in the town he wrecked.

For better or worse, William Clarke Quantrill and his guerrilla army will be forever linked to Lawrence, Kansas. On the morning of August 21, 1863, they charged into the town and killed some 180 men and boys and set fire to their homes. They failed to get their No. 1 target, Jim Lane, who fled into a cornfield in his nightshirt the moment he heard the first gunshots. But hey, at least they didn't dishonor themselves by harming any women — a perverse point of honor for Quantrill after the Union Prison Collapse killed four female Bushwhackers (see page 148).

In researching this guide we were surprised to find no permanent public space for learning about this infamous raid, other than the

"Old Sacramento," which was fired in celebration of Kansas statehood in 1861, then stolen in the Liberty Arsenal raid two months later, at the Watkins Community Museum.

Lawrence Visitor Center (see below), two dioramas at the Lone Jack Civil War Museum (page 143) and a small exhibit at the Burnt District Museum (page 156). But now the Douglas County Historical Society's museum, located in the historic Watkins Bank in downtown Lawrence, is undergoing a multi-stage renovation that will include a new permanent exhibit on the Civil War years.

The exhibit, which we were able to preview, will begin in the restored bank lobby on the first floor. Turning left, visitors will immediately spot Ernst Ulmer's arresting 1990 painting of Quantrill's raid, part of the museum's collection. Behind that will be a new gallery that increases the space devoted to the events that gripped the nation in the 1850s and '60s. We hope the Watkins will follow the example of the Burnt District Museum and link the raid in Lawrence to the issuance a few days later of General Order No. 11. This Army edict, as we discussed in the introduction to this chapter, forced 20,000 people off their farms, caused untold suffering, and reaped bitter fruit for generations to come.

Lawrence Visitor Center ❸
Lawrence, Kansas (402 North 2nd Street)

Visitor center with documentary film. Hours: 8:30 to 5:30 Monday thru Saturday, May to September, 9 to 5 in the off-season; open 1 to 5 Sundays year-round. **Free.** ⑥: Yes. Who runs it: Lawrence Convention & Visitors Bureau (visitlawrence.com). ℄ 785-856-3040.

 Our Take
Historical film and helpful staff make for a superior VC.

Ang Lee's film *Ride with the Devil* is still, in our view, the best way to relive the Lawrence massacre (see "Book and Film Suggestions," page 228). But we also liked the locally-produced 27-minute film on Quantrill's Raid playing at the Lawrence Visitors Center. Located in a renovated Union Pacific depot (trains still roar by throughout the day but don't stop), the center has racks upon racks of maps and brochures from around Kansas. Ask for the self-guided tours of the places in Douglas County raided by Quantrill's men, or of the homes in historic West Lawrence. We have found the staff eager to help visitors make the most of their history travels.

Burnt District Museum ⑩

Harrisonville, Missouri (400 East Mechanic, upper level)

One-room museum. Hours: 10 to 3:30 weekdays. **Free.** &: Yes. Who runs it: Cass County Historical Society. ✆ 816-380-4396.

 Our Take

Solid niche source of information about the Burnt District and Quantrill's Raid from a local point of view.

Cass County saw it all in the Civil War: regimental battles, guerrilla warfare, and the near-complete devastation wreaked by General Order No. 11. We were surprised to see all of this covered inside a small L-shaped room that is essentially a shared office with the Cass County Historical Society.

The fighting never rose above skirmishes, though a raid by Jim Lane's Brigade on September 17, 1861, devastated Morristown, as depicted in a diorama at the museum done by a local couple. A record book from 1874 details claims recorded by county residents whose property was destroyed or confiscated as a result of Order No. 11. Most of these claims — $60 for lost hay, $400 for a house — were never settled.

There is a not-bad dramatized audio program that plays from behind life-sized cutouts of Quantrill and Cole Younger, a Cass County native and fellow guerrilla. Recounting the Lawrence raid one of them says, "Many old scores were settled that night." Of course they were not, and Younger, who would live into his seventies, would one day renounce the actions of his youth.

Burnt District Monument ⑪

Harrisonville, Missouri (2501 W. Wall at the Cass County Justice Center)

Monument. Free. &: Yes. Info: Cass County Historical Society. ✆ 816-380-4396.

 Our Take

Outstanding as public art as well as public memory.

In our time touring Civil War battlefields and other historic sites, we have seen a lot of statues of heroes in heroic poses, oversized

"Jennison's tombstones" inspired both the Burnt District Monument (left) and Tom Lea's 1939 mural at the Pleasant Hill Post Office.

plaques overflowing with words, and memorial stones of every shape and size. What we had never seen before — and never expected to find so moving — was a chimney monument.

The Burnt District Monument is a memorial recently erected to the thousands of people whose homes were burned to the ground in the area that was cleared out after the enforcement of General Order No. 11. Union soldiers and Kansas "Red Legs" torched many houses; others were lost in unattended grass fires. Only the stone chimneys remained. They became known as "Jennison's tombstones," after Jayhawker Charles "Doc" Jennison.

The Jayhawkers also ransacked the Missourians' homes for plunder, sometimes not even waiting until the occupants had departed. And the fields were burned to prevent Bushwhackers from foraging on them. Confederate guerrillas retaliated by burning the Unionist homes that were left standing — its occupants had moved closer to the Federal garrisons in the area. All told, at least 20,000 people were displaced by Order No. 11.

The monument is an imposing stone chimney that was handcrafted using traditional tools by local stonemasons Jerry and Jarrod Saling.

Some of the rock used in the monument was acquired from the Henry W. Younger farm nearby, thus providing a direct link to the history of the Burnt District, as four of the Younger brothers would become Confederate guerrillas and later outlaws with Jesse James. Inset plaques on three sides summarize the story of Order No. 11. Stone benches are nearby for contemplation. The surrounding area has been planted with native trees, shrubs, and prairie grasses.

Pleasant Hill Post Office ❾
Pleasant Hill, Missouri (124 Veterans Parkway)

Lobby mural. Hours: 24/7, daytime better for viewing. **Free.** ♿: Yes.

 Our Take
Striking New Deal-era depiction of the Burnt District.

Tom Lea (1907–2001) would become a renowned illustrator for *Life* magazine during World War II, publish bestselling novels and histories, and command top dollar for his paintings. But in 1939 the El Paso native was just getting through the Depression when he received a federal contract to paint a mural at the Pleasant Hill Post Office. As he worked, he listened to the radio. Troubled by what he called "the daily blasts of bad news from Europe," Lea decided to paint "some forlorn people standing on a piece of desolated ground, after a war." Featured prominently was a burnt chimney. He titled it *Back Home, April, 1865*.

The four adults in the picture are looking in different directions, symbolizing their temporal relation to the carnage. The mother, clutching her infant, stares defiantly forward.

Baxter Springs Heritage Center ⑯
Baxter Springs, Kansas (740 East Avenue)

Sprawling but well-organized community museum. Hours: 10 to 4:30 Monday thru Saturday, 1 to 4:30 Sunday. **Free.** ♿: Yes; no elevator but lower level has drive-up doors. Who runs it: Baxter Springs Historical Society (baxterspringsmuseum.org). ☎ 620-856-2385.

Memorial to Quantrill's massacre victims at Baxter Springs.

🗨 Our Take

Interesting gallery of Civil War exhibits is only one part of
this large museum full of local memories.

Fort Blair wasn't much more than a log-and-earth cantonment in
southeastern Kansas when, in the fall of 1863, William Quantrill's
guerrillas attacked it. They were repulsed by soldiers from the
Second Kansas Colored Volunteer Infantry, but as the raiders rode
out of Baxter Springs they took a Union wagon train by surprise.
General James G. Blunt escaped, but 100 out of 185 Federals were
massacred, including the unarmed members of a military band and
the black drummer boy.

Local artist Ed Ness, who was inspired by the paintings of Thomas
Hart Benton (see page 206), created a 7-by-12-foot mural of
the scene. It's part of a section of Civil War exhibits that is both
substantial and a small fraction of what the Baxter Springs
Historical Society has on display at this two-story, 20,000-square-
foot museum.

Seemingly no aspect of the community's history is left untold.
Notable are the exhibits on the area mining industry, the town's
stellar baseball legacy, and, since Baxter Springs is on Route 66, the
obligatory America's Road exhibit. On the museum's website is a list
of ten tours you can request from one of the dedicated volunteers.

Soldiers' Lot: Two miles west of town is the cemetery containing the Soldiers' Lot where victims of the Baxter Springs massacre were buried. Its impressive marble and granite memorial was dedicated to the memory of the fallen.

Local color: Don't pass up the **Route 66 Visitor Center** (page 223).

Near here: Joplin, Neosho, and Diamond are just across the state line in Missouri (see Index).

Local Museum Spotlight

Clay County Museum ❶
Liberty, Missouri (14 North Main Street on the courthouse square). Hours: 1 to 4 weekdays, 10 to 4 Saturdays; closed in January. Suggested donation $3. ♿: First floor only. Who runs it: the Historical Society (claycountymuseum.org). Phone: 816-792-1849.

 Our Take

> Steps from Liberty Jail and Jesse James Bank Museum, it's worth dropping by to see the mural and other items.

Located right on Liberty's courthouse square and housed in an 1865 building that served as a drugstore and doctors' offices, this collection of local history focuses on the area's connection with "Little Dixie" — the Southern-sympathizing counties of Missouri that lie south of the Missouri River. On the upper floor, an early 20th-century mural of the region's history adds interest.

Bates County Museum ⓭
Butler, Missouri (802 Elks Drive. Follow Sunset Drive north of Highway 52, then right on Mill Street) Hours: 9:30 to 4 Tuesday thru Friday and 9:30 to noon Saturday, April to October. **Free.** ♿: Yes. Who runs it: Bates County Historical Society (batescountymuseum.org). ☎ 660-679-0134.

 Our Take

> Civil War (and Robert Heinlein) aficionados, stop here.

The Bates County Museum is developing interpretive signs to

Confederate Gen. J.O. Shelby, one of Missouri's largest slaveholders, is honored in a mural at the Bates County Museum ... right next to a mural of African-American soldiers fighting at Island Mound.

accompany its already large collection of donated objects. For instance, visitors can learn here about the ongoing archaeological digs conducted by Ann M. Raab that are helping historians and others to better understand how the Civil War affected the lives of Bates County residents.

On the second floor is an arresting trio of murals that pays tribute to heroes on both sides — the soldiers at Island Mound and a local legend, Confederate general J.O. Shelby. A timeline traces the history of the county from the ill-fated Harmony Mission in 1821 forward. There's plenty else to see in the museum, including Victorian period rooms, an exhibit on Robert Heinlein — the pioneering science fiction author and free thinker who was born and raised in Butler — and a display about the Minuteman missiles that were once siloed around the county during the Cold War.

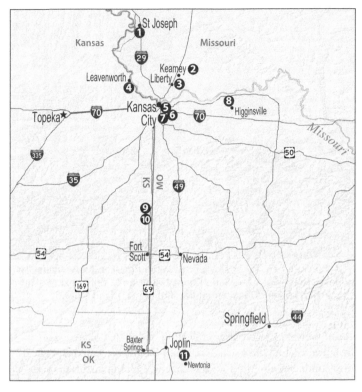

Sites in This Chapter

Tip: The Orientation Map on page 248 shows all Big Divide towns.

A visitor standing at the Union monument in Springfield National Cemetery cannot see this monument to Missouri Confederates.

From Price's Raid to Jesse James

Something happened after Quantrill's Raiders went crazy in Lawrence and Baxter Springs. According to author Edward Leslie, "Quantrill's 'old men' — who had been with him since the early days — were dismayed by the breakdown in discipline and the escalating violence." Over the winter in Texas, these once-trusted lieutenants "said their good-byes and slipped away," leaving Quantrill vulnerable. In time his authority was challenged and control of the most feared guerrilla band in the country passed to its two most ruthless killers, "Bloody Bill" Anderson and George Todd. (Union troops shot Quantrill in Kentucky in 1865.)

By early 1864 the Confederate Army had ended the Partisan Ranger experiment with the blessing of Gen. Robert E. Lee, who complained that "it is almost impossible, under the best officers even, to have discipline in these bands." But many in "Little Dixie" and western Missouri continued to support the Bushwhackers. They felt the guerrillas were the only ones taking the fight to the Federal occupiers who had made their lives miserable.

By the summer of 1864 two of Lee's generals, Sterling Price and J.O. Shelby, wanted another chance to win Missouri for the Confederacy. They believed the state was rife with pro-Southern feeling and that if they made a show of force, the people would rise up and join their insurrection. Shelby had led a cavalry raid into Missouri the previous fall that had done great damage to Union strongholds. He came away convinced that the state was theirs for the taking. With Atlanta having fallen on September 2, Jefferson Davis was willing to consider anything that could harm Lincoln's chances for re-election and lead to the North suing for peace.

And so, on September 19 Price and Shelby rode north from Arkansas equipped with 12,000 cavalry, 14 cannon, and a large wagon train for bringing plunder back to the South. The campaign started badly, as Price let himself be tempted by a small and tactically unimportant garrison near Pilot Knob in southeastern Missouri. Though the Confederates vastly outnumbered the Union forces inside the fort — which included Gen. Thomas Ewing of Order No. 11 infamy — Price's men launched uncoordinated attacks that Ewing's men repulsed while inflicting 1,000 casualties on the rebel army. Adding insult to injury, many in Price's ranks fled, never to return, and Ewing managed to get everyone out of the fort

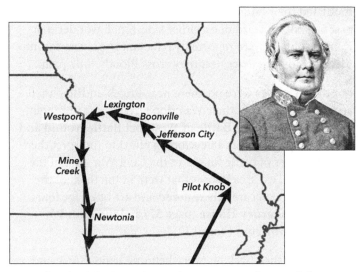

After the debacle at Pilot Knob, Price (pictured) steered clear of trouble until his forces reached Westport.

safely at night while the rebels slept.

Having lost the element of surprise, Price turned away from St. Louis and instead worked his way west across the state, a long slog that further thinned his ranks through illness and defections. As for the people rising up, few did, except in anger at marauding Confederates in Price's army who seemed less interested in fighting than in stealing from the homes and farms of civilians without regard to political leanings.

Outside Jefferson City, Price had a friendly meeting with the guerrillas and deputized them in service of the Confederate Army. Then he sent them off to wreak havoc in almost the opposite direction of his army. This was fine with Anderson and Todd, who had been delivering their special brand of justice all summer long and would continue to do so during Price's raid. Of their more than 20 guerrilla raids in 1864, the sickest and bloodiest took place on September 24 in Centralia, where Anderson's men slaughtered 150 Union troops, mutilated their bodies and took their victims' scalps — a practice not unheard of on either side. Small wonder that Kansas soldiers were reportedly reluctant to go very far into Missouri to fight Price, lest they cross Bloody Bill's path.

But the guerrillas were nowhere near Price's undisciplined army when they met their Waterloo at Westport in present-day Kansas City. **The Battle of Westport Battleground and Museum** (page 169) is a developing effort to interpret the largest theater of battle fought in the Civil War west of the Mississippi. Two area houses that were in the thick of the action have been carefully restored and are open for tours: the **Harris-Kearney House** (page 57) and the **John Wornall House Museum** (page 170).

Price was pushed back by overwhelming Union force and was saved from likely capture only because of a daring rear-guard action by Shelby, one of the Civil War's great characters and instinctive fighters. After Westport, the rebels retreated south. Price's wagon train, seriously loaded down with goods, was about to cost him dearly. Just across the state line in Kansas, two smaller Union divisions caught up with the Confederates and routed them at what is now the **Mine Creek Battlefield State Historic Site** (page 171).

Painter H.C. Wyeth's depiction of the Battle of Westport is on display at the Missouri State Capitol in Jefferson City.

The Federals continued to pursue the rebels through southwest Missouri. To pick up speed, Price burned much of his supply train. At the **Second Battle of Newtonia** (page 144), Shelby once more came to the rescue, dismounting at the Confederates' rear and firing at Union forces. This audacious move allowed what was left of Price's army to stagger back to Arkansas. The West was in the Union Army's hands for good.

The Missouri-Kansas border region suffered as terribly from four years of war as any area. Missouri had more skirmishes and battles fought on its soil than any state other than Virginia and Tennessee, and many communities were burned out entirely. Thousands of Unionist Missourians were forced to seek refuge in Federal garrisons or flee to Kansas for the duration of the war. As for Kansas, its soldiers had the highest casualty rate of any state in the Union. In 1862 Congress, having realized there would be staggering loss of life, established fourteen **national cemeteries**, including Springfield, Missouri (page 113) and Forts Leavenworth and Scott, Kansas (page 173). Hundreds more cemeteries and **soldiers' lots** — portions of existing cemeteries cordoned off for the military dead — were commissioned nationwide in places like Mound City (page 172) and Baxter Springs, Kansas (page 158). **Union Cemetery** in Kansas City was later designated for a Confederate memorial (page 172).

Over time countless bodies would be exhumed from their original burial spots, transported, and re-interred in places of honor, a migration of the dead engineered by a grieving and restless nation. The very last bones to be displaced were those of the notorious William Clarke Quantrill, whose partial remains were re-interred in 1992 at the **Confederate Memorial State Historic Site** in Higginsville, Missouri (page 174).

In writing this book, our plan had been to include the three historic Jesse James-related sites (two of which are outstanding) in the next chapter, "After the War." The public, after all, did not know who Jesse or his brother Frank James were until

Jesse James' gang was defined by their bitter refusal to accept the outcome of the war.

1870, long after rebel soldiers had put down their guns. But as we visited these sites, we saw how the story of the James gang was completely tied up in Missouri's Civil War. Jesse's hatred of the Union had been seared into him as a 15-year-old during an incident on the **James Farm** (page 175). The violent acts he and Frank committed after the war were an extension of the politically motivated cruelty they had learned under the tutelage of "Bloody Bill" Anderson. Their anger at the Union Army for killing their friends — including guerrilla leaders Anderson and Todd, who were ambushed as Price retreated from Missouri — led Frank, Jesse, and the Youngers to continue their Bushwhacking long after Appomattox.

In his book *Jesse James: Last Rebel of the Civil War,* T.J. Stiles argues that the James gang's reign of terror was defined by their bitter refusal to accept the outcome of the war. Everything can be seen through this lens — from the choice of banks they robbed (**Jesse James Bank Museum**, page 176) to the bounty put on Jesse's head by the Unionist governor of Missouri, which led Bob Ford to pull the trigger at the **Jesse James Home** (page 176). And the gang's celebrity status suggested that lots of people in Missouri and elsewhere felt the same way they did.

As Stiles put it, "the James story shows how the legacy of the Civil War was a powerful force in and of itself for decades after it ended."

Battle of Westport Visitor Center ❻

Kansas City, Missouri (6601 Swope Parkway at Meyer Boulevard)

Visitor center and museum. Open 1 to 5 Thursday thru Saturday, April to October. **Free.** ♿: Yes. Operated by Monnett Battle of Westport Fund (battleofwestport.org/visitorcenter). ✆ 913-345-2000 (ask for Dan Smith).

 Our Take

We urge everyone to learn more about the largest battle in the Civil War west of the Mississippi.

Near this visitor center is one of the last great undeveloped battlefields of the Civil War — rated Class A for its strategic importance, but until recently little more than a languishing industrial area with historical markers.

In late 1864 the Confederate Army allowed Sterling Price to stage one last invasion of his home state, where three years prior he had prevailed at Lexington and Wilson's Creek. Alas, Price's Raid was doomed from the start. By the time his army limped into present-day Kansas City on October 21, 1864, his 12,000-man cavalry brigade had been cut in half.

Gen. Samuel R. Curtis knew Price was coming and was able to amass a nearly three-to-one advantage using Kansas state militia, Union troops under James G. Blunt and cavalry under Alfred Pleasonton. Finding himself sandwiched between Curtis to the west and Pleasonton, Price tried attacking Curtis's mile-long flank, but it held. With Pleasonton pressing and disaster looming, Price was forced to escape to the south, with Shelby covering his rear — in more ways than one.

There is a Battle of Westport auto tour, with some two dozen historical markers erected around town by the Native Sons and Daughters of Kansas City. That's a lot of markers, and unfortunately most are in the urban core surrounded by asphalt. (One exception is Jacob I. Loose Park, about a mile north of the John Wornall House Museum, listed below. At the park's south end the historical marker is augmented by interpretive signage and cannon to give a better sense of the action.)

Over the years local preservationists have been working on purchasing and clearing a portion of the Big Blue battlefield that includes Byram's Ford, a river crossing that played a major role in the battle. The hope is to complete battlefield restoration in time for its sesquicentennial in 2014. For now, there is the visitor center with the helpful volunteer to walk you through the exhibits and battle artifacts. We encourage any traveler with interest in the Civil War to visit.

☛ **Battle casualties:** Union 1,500 of 22,000 (7 percent), Confederate 1,500 of 8,500 (18 percent).

John Wornall House Museum ❼
Kansas City, Missouri (6115 Wornall Road)

Historic home. Tours 10 to 3 Tuesday thru Saturday, 1 to 3 Sunday. Tours are $6 for adults, $5 for seniors and children 6-12. ♿: First floor, plus photos of second floor. Who runs it: Privately operated. ☎ 816-444-1858.

 Our Take

Many 1850s delights in this restored home that was in the thick of it during the Battle of Westport.

This Greek Revival-style home was built for the family of John Wornall, a civic-minded and prosperous farmer-businessman originally from Kentucky. After his first wife died, he married Eliza

The John Wornall House is one of more than two dozen sites adorned with historic markers for its role in the Battle of Westport.

Johnson, daughter of the couple who founded the Shawnee Indian Mission (page 39). The Wornalls' house is furnished much the same way it was in their time, with the furniture, decorative arts, and appliances of a wealthy antebellum western home.

You've probably never wondered what style of chair President Lincoln was sitting in at Ford's Theater the night he was shot, but the family had one just like it and it's here. Indeed, our guide was a trove of Wornall lore, including the grim details about the Civil War "medicine" dispensed inside while the Battle of Westport raged outside. An excellent website complements your visit with additional information on the house, its occupants, and the times.

Mine Creek Battlefield State Historic Site ⑩

near Pleasanton, Kansas (20485 Highway 52, just west of US-71)

★ A Big Divide Top Site ★

Large battlefield with visitor center. Hours: 10 to 5 Wednesday thru Saturday, April to October only. Admission: $5 for adults, $1 students. Walking trail is open year-round. ♿: Museum yes; mowed turf on trail is challenging. Who runs it: Kansas Historical Society (kshs.org). ✆ 913-352-8890.

 Our Take

Prairie path immerses you in the only major Civil War battle in Kansas and one of the war's biggest cavalry charges.

The end was nigh for Sterling Price. A small force under Union general Alfred Pleasonton had chased Price's army from Westport south to a skirmish at Marais des Cygnes. Though outnumbered, Pleasonton's men were well-rested and well-armed. Finally, at Mine Creek, the long Confederate wagon train — laden with plundered supplies needed by the South — got mired in the mud.

In one of the largest cavalry engagements of the Civil War, Pleasonton moved aggressively, inflicting heavy casualties. Two Confederate generals and 600 soldiers surrendered; the rest fled.

Local preservationists, working with the Civil War Battlefield Trust, have been able to purchase and restore a large portion of the Mine Creek field. There is a modern visitor center and 2.6 miles of trails,

Interpretive walking trail at Mine Creek Battlefield site.

including a half-mile loop through the tallgrass with interesting signage. Along the walking paths, you start to take in the scene of Price's desperate retreat, with hundreds of wagons struggling to ford the creek while Union troops attacked.

☞ **Battle casualties:** Union 100 of 2,600 (0.2 percent), Confederate 1,200 of 7,000 (17 percent).

☞ **Soldiers' lot:** Many of the dead from Mine Creek were eventually interred at the **Mound City Soldiers' Lot**. Both site are on our Highway 52 tour (page 131).

Union Cemetery ❺

Kansas City, Missouri (227 East 28th Terrace, south of Crown Center)

Cemetery. Open 8 to 3 weekdays or by appointment. Sexton cottage open 11 to 3 Friday. ♿: No. Who runs it: Union Cemetery Historical Society. ✆ 816-472-4990.

 Our Take

One of the area's oldest and more unusual cemeteries.

Union was named not for the winning side in the Civil War but for the fact that way back when, there were two towns named Kansas City and Westport and they went in together on a cemetery. Now in the heart of the Kansas City metro area and located just south of downtown, this eclectic boneyard has 55,000 graves and tombs, along with picnic tables and a well-marked self-guided tour (maps are available from the sexton's cottage).

Among the notables buried here are a number of the city's early founders as well as the painter George Caleb Bingham (see page 150). Fifteen Confederate prisoners of war from the Battle of Westport are also here — exactly where, no one is quite sure, but their names are listed on bronze tablets in the northeast corner of the cemetery.

Ft. Leavenworth Nat'l Cemetery/Ft. Sully ❹

Fort Leavenworth, Kansas (395 Biddle Boulevard). © 913-758-4105.

 Our Take

Older than Arlington, Fort Leavenworth's cemetery was built atop African American history.

Fort Leavenworth was founded in 1827 and, along with Fort Scott, was designated a National Cemetery in 1862, two years before Congress created one in Arlington, Va. Some of the victims from Quantrill's Lawrence Raid are buried here, as are seven Confederate prisoners of war. After the war Union soldiers from Kansas City, St. Joseph, and Independence were reinterred here, as were the remains of Henry Leavenworth, the fort's first commander, nearly 70 years after his death.

Before the cemetery was situated here a small garrison called **Fort Sully** was built along the highest elevation and defended during the Civil War by 256 black soldiers. There is a Fort Sully marker in the cemetery on the west side of Biddle; it is included on the African-American driving tour map available at the **Frontier Army Museum** (page 34). Fort Leavenworth requires a valid photo ID and car inspection for entry.

☛ **Fort Scott National Cemetery:** Fort Scott National Cemetery is maintained by Fort Leavenworth. It sits on a manicured slope about a mile from Fort Scott National Historic Site (page 40). A monument toward the crest of the hill pays tribute to the First Kansas Colored Infantry of Island Mound fame (page 146).

Confederate Memorial State Historic Site ❽

Higginsville, Missouri (211 W. First Street)

Park with visitor center, historic chapel, and cemetery. Hours: Park is open dawn to dusk. Buildings are kept open 8 to 4 Thursday thru Saturday, noon to 5 Sunday, April to September; shorter hours October to March. **Free.** ♿: Chapel, visitor center, and one fishing pond. Who runs it: Missouri State Parks (mostateparks.com). ✆ 660-584-2853.

💬 Our Take

Historic park has an interesting post-Civil War story.

Because veterans of the rebel army were not eligible for federal pensions, the Confederate Soldiers' Home was established with private money to serve their needs. Some 1,600 veterans, many of them disabled or still suffering from wounds received during the Civil War, became residents of the home set on prime farmland near Higginsville, Missouri, from 1891 to 1950. In 1897 the state took financial control of the home, and after the last veteran died the site was turned into a 135-acre public park with fishing ponds, walking and biking trails, and picnic grounds as well as historical buildings.

Parts of Quantrill's remains were buried following a memorial at the chapel. (His skull is still in Ohio.)

Rangers give guided tours at no charge, but these must be reserved in advance. Otherwise, start at the ranger's office across from the chapel and cemetery. Knock on the door to your left as you enter and request to see the well-done orientation video. Then cross the road to tour the cemetery and restored chapel. Interpretive signage explains, among other things, why the U.S. flag is flown at a rebel graveyard, a source of controversy some years back.

Speaking of controversy, the chapel played host to a memorial service for William Clarke Quantrill in 1992. Why so late? Some of his remains had just been acquired by the Sons of Confederate Veterans. They were then laid to rest in the cemetery following a memorial service attended by hundreds (many in period dress). The ceremony capped more than a century of disputation over Quantrill's bones, some of which were still in his original Kentucky grave. Your guide will be happy to tell the full story, including why Quantrill's skull is not in Missouri or Kentucky, but in Ohio.

Jesse James Farm and Museum ❷
★ A Big Divide Top Site ★

Kearney, Missouri (21216 Jesse James Farm Road)

Historic homestead and visitor center. Open 9 to 4 daily, May to September; noon to 4 Sundays in the off-season. Admission $8 adults, $7 seniors, $4.50 children 8-17. ♿: Yes. Who runs it: Clay County. ✆ 816-736-8500.

 Our Take

If you're looking for the real Jesse James, his boyhood home is as close as you'll get.

Born in 1847 to a Baptist minister and his flinty wife Zerelda, Jesse James, along with his brother Frank, were raised in a God-fearing, pro-Southern household. When Frank left to join Confederate guerrillas in 1863, Union soldiers brutalized Jesse and his stepfather, seeking Frank's whereabouts. By 1864 the vengeance-seeking 16-year-old was riding with "Bloody Bill" Anderson and taking part in the massacre at Centralia, Missouri. After the Civil War Jesse and Frank, along with the Younger brothers, started their own private war. Their robbery-murders were always tinged with political motives — to punish Missourians who had been loyal to the Union in the war and to avenge the deaths of their guerrilla friends. Thanks to excellent publicity from a Kansas City journalist, the James gang became folk heroes, earning unwarranted comparisons to Robin Hood.

Thanks to Clay County residents, the James farm was saved and turned into a first-rate museum with the largest collection of authentic James family items, including the boots Jesse was wearing when he was shot, a cache of weapons, crazy quilts made by women in his family, and Jesse's original coffin. Tours are included in the price of the ticket. A winding path leads to the restored James farmhouse and Jesse's onetime gravesite (which Zerelda used to charge admission to view).

Jesse James Home Museum ❶
St. Joseph, Missouri (701 Messanie Street, next door to Patee House)

Historic site. Open 10 to 4:30 Monday thru Saturday and 1 to 4:30 Sunday, April to October; off-season hours vary so call ahead. Admission $4 adults, $3 seniors, $2 ages 6-17. Ⓑ: Yes. Who runs it: Pony Express Historical Association. ☎ 816-232-8206.

 Our Take
Strictly for Jesse aficionados.

This four-room house has been a magnet for curiosity seekers almost from the moment that Jesse James was shot and killed here by Bob Ford, a member of his own gang who hoped to collect a $10,000 bounty. The structure has since been hauled to its current location, next to Patee House; both museums are under the same ownership. Your short tour will include looking at news stories about the shooting and recent exhumation of Jesse's body, listening to a short audio program, and examining the framed hole-in-the-wall where a bullet supposedly lodged after passing through Jesse's skull (though an autopsy has suggested that there was no exit wound). Admission is a separate fee from the Patee House Museum next door, meaning that it will appeal largely to visitors who can't get enough of Jesse James and his legend.

Jesse James Bank Museum ❸
Liberty, Missouri (103 North Water Street, across from courthouse square)

Historic site. Hours: 10 to 4 Monday thru Saturday. Tours are $6 for adults, $5.50 seniors, $3.50 children 8+. Ⓑ: Yes. Who runs it: Clay County, Missouri. ☎ 816-736-8510.

 Our Take

An enjoyable you-are-there experience — even if Jesse and Frank didn't rob the bank.

On February 13, 1866, armed men came into this building and pulled off the first daylight bank robbery in U.S. history. Upon escaping, they killed one innocent bystander and wounded another. There is no proof that Jesse James, Frank James, or members of their gang were involved in the robbery, but the evidence points that way — at least in hindsight. The bank lost $62,000, almost everything it had in assets, and was forced to close its doors.

The bank museum is meant to take the visitor back to the moment when the robbery went down. The Seth Thomas wall clock is even set to the exact time of the heist. The original green vault is still there, standing open and unprotected. Our guide was knowledgeable and committed to telling the story as faithfully as possible from the banker's report, made only an hour after the robbery. The back room in the museum is devoted to the legends and mischaracterizations of Jesse James in books and movies. There's also a small gift shop.

Local Museum Spotlight

Linn County Historical Museum ❾

Pleasanton, Kansas (307 East Park Street). Open 9 to 5 Tuesday and Thursday, 1 to 5 weekends. **Free.** ♿: Yes. ✆ 913-352-8739.

Our Take

Nicely interpreted county museum.

The entry exhibit takes you through the early history of eastern Kansas, the first settlers and Indians, and exhibits on the area's two major claims to fame: the Marais des Cygnes Massacre and the Battle of Mine Creek. Longtime museum director Ola May Earnest has created a tidy, well-organized space with some strong interpretive touches, like a lighted battle map and audio program on the Battle of Mine Creek to go with a spiffy classic-car collection and a well-stocked genealogical library.

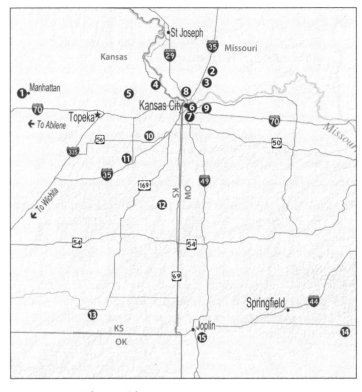

Sites in This Chapter

Tip: The Index lists all sites in every town.

The Hannibal and St. Joseph Railroad Bridge in Kansas City (pictured in the late 1800s) was the first rail span across the Missouri River.

∽∾ 8 ∽∾
After the War

For generations the death toll of the four-year Civil War was set at 620,000 — more than all the deaths in all the other wars in U.S. history combined. Incredibly, scholars now believe that number was too low. Using newly-acquired census data, historians have revised that number upward, to three quarters of a million Americans dead, from battlefield wounds, infections, and disease.

For the living, the return to civilian life would be a formidable struggle in places. Missouri's countryside lay in shambles.

Of those forced to evacuate the four counties affected by General Order No. 11, only an estimated 40 percent ever returned. Those who did faced mind-boggling challenges of recovery — including tax bills for the three years they had been absent. Loyalty oaths were administered, and those who would not take them, or had worn the gray in battle, saw many opportunities closed off to them.

The great majority of Missourians were simply trying to rebuild their lives and communities. One of the most successful ventures from that time was a textile factory whose skilled workers lived nearby in a self-sufficient village called Bethany Plantation. Remarkably, the mill survived virtually intact and is now one of The Big Divide's unique destinations, **Watkins Woolen Mill State Historic Site** (page 185).

Gaining the vote in 1870 did not put bread on the table for the black men who had distinguished themselves by their military service in the war. So, some stayed in the army, re-enlisting as part of a new division of African-American soldiers charged with patrolling the wide-open West. These "Buffalo Soldiers" are the focus of the **Richard Allen Cultural Center** in Leavenworth, Kansas (page 184), and a splendid monument inside Fort Leavenworth that was instigated by the base's then-deputy commander, Colin Powell (see Frontier Army Museum, page 34).

Members of the 25th Infantry "Buffalo Soldiers," stationed at Fort Keogh in Montana in 1890. Some are wearing buffalo robes.

Even the historic sites in the border region that appeared to have little to do with the Civil War were in fact inextricably tied to, delayed by, or shaped by the great conflict.

The transcontinental railroad, for instance, was the catalyst for the Kansas-Nebraska Act in 1854, even though it took another fifteen years, until 1869, to make the cross-country line a reality. Two months after the driving of the "golden spike" in Utah, history was made again as enterprising businessmen in Kansas City completed the first rail span across the Missouri River. The Hannibal Bridge turned the city overnight into the region's preeminent transportation hub, a fact celebrated by the **Town of Kansas Bridge** (page 187).

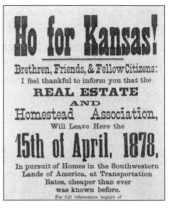

Ho for Kansas!

Brethren, Friends, & Fellow Citizens:

I feel thankful to inform you that the

REAL ESTATE

AND

Homestead Association,

Will Leave Here the

15th of April, 1878,

In pursuit of Homes in the Southwestern Lands of America, at Transportation Rates, cheaper than ever was known before.

For full information inquire of

Congress amended the Homestead Act so that women and former slaves could also own land.

The homestead movement also has a Civil War legacy. Though it flourished in the 1870s and 1880s, it really should have gotten underway in the mid-1850s with the opening of Kansas and Nebraska territories. Instead, the Homestead Act was held up for years by pro-slavery senators, who wished to deny Free Soilers this last triumph in the battle over popular sovereignty in Kansas. "Better for us," a pro-slavery newspaper declared, "that these territories should remain a waste, a howling wilderness, trod only by red hunters than be so settled."

Finally in 1862, with the Southern roadblock gone, Congress passed the Homestead Act, but with some important changes: Women and former slaves, as well as white men, would be able to "prove up" their 160 acres of land and secure its title. No one, however, who had taken up arms against the U.S. Government would be granted a claim.

Laura Ingalls Wilder was a late bloomer.

The Homestead Act unleashed a generation of land-seekers onto the Plains, none more famous than Charles Ingalls — "Pa" of the beloved series of books written by his second child, Laura Ingalls Wilder. The best known Wilder book, *Little House on the Prairie*, is set in southeastern Kansas in a log cabin not unlike the replica at the **Little House on the Prairie Museum** near Independence, Kansas (page 189). Across the state line in Mansfield, Missouri, is the **Laura Ingalls Wilder Home** (page 188), where this retired teacher in her sixties, with encouragement from her journalist daughter, began to write all those books.

The same year that the Ingalls family moved to Kansas, the residents of Johnson County, Kansas, built a one-room schoolhouse of native fieldstone and named it for the infamous Jayhawker James H. Lane. The country schoolhouse is a staple of rural historical museums, but Lanesfield's 93 years of continuous service, and efforts by an affluent suburban county to preserve it, put **Lanesfield School** (page 189) and the modern, well-interpreted museum next door in a class of their own.

The man most responsible for improving early education in Kansas — for girls as well as boys — was the abolitionist

Isaac Goodnow, founder of the state teachers' association and its college (**Goodnow House State Historic Site**, page 190). In 1862, Congress passed the Morrill Act, another bill that had been held up by Southern resistance, authorizing land set-asides for higher education. The following year, the teachers' college would become the nation's first land-grant school, known today as Kansas State University.

African Americans gained citizenship and with it the promise of new opportunities of public education. But Jim Crow laws and extensive discrimination — both in the North and South — created new barriers and challenges.

One of the most successful challengers to racial stereotypes was the scientist and inventor George Washington Carver. Born into slavery during the Civil War, Carver doggedly pursued learning, overcoming numerous imposing setbacks because of his race. All of this is inspirationally recounted at the **George Washington Carver National Monument** (page 191), one of our Big Divide Top Sites.

As the century came to a close, railroads continued to be the driver for economic development in hundreds of towns stretching out into the hinterlands. Small wonder that so many of these towns later converted their handsome railroad depots into cultural centers. The $175 million restoration of Kansas City's **Union Station** (page 194), which also restored Amtrak service to the station, is a breathtaking case. But we were also impressed by the more modest efforts in Ottawa, Kansas, to turn its railroad depot into a community museum (**Old Depot Museum,** page 195).

In this chapter we end by highlighting three "towns" assembled from authentic period buildings in their communities and a one-of-a-kind place, **Leila's Hair Museum** (page 195), that is all about Victorian-era hair art.

Prints from the Everhard Collection, featuring portraits of post-Civil War African Americans in Kansas, line the walls of the Richard Allen Cultural Center. Above, Geraldine Jones of Leavenworth in 1910.

Richard Allen Cultural Center ❹
Leavenworth, Kansas (412 Kiowa)

Museum. Hours: 1 to 6 weekdays, 10 to 1 Saturday, or by appointment. Suggested donation $5. ♿: Yes. Privately operated. ☏ 913-682-8772.

 Our Take

Inspiring museum features Buffalo Soldiers and the region's African-American achievers.

Phyllis Bass has been the heart and soul of this community museum since it opened in 1992. On both our visits she was our tour guide, and she patiently walked us through every display case and exhibit in this museum, highlighting the achievements and success of African Americans in everything from medicine to military affairs. The museum is attached to a house originally owned by one of Leavenworth's first black cavalrymen — the "Buffalo Soldiers," formed in 1866, integrated into the regular army in 1952, and preserved here for all time.

She talked about the Buffalo Soldiers and the sculptor Eddie Dixon who created the monument at Fort Leavenworth that its then-deputy commander, Colin Powell, had demanded to honor the African-American men who paved the way for the likes of himself.

We couldn't help noticing that the majestic "Black Dignity" photos, from the renowned collection of local photographer Mary Ellen Everhard, were displayed beside pictures of lynchings and a Klan parade through downtown Leavenworth. From time to time during our tour, we saw sobering reminders of black Kansans succeeding despite widespread racism.

Other artifacts worth seeing here: "freedom papers" of formal emancipation, signed by General Samuel Curtis in 1863; leg chains belonging to a slave master; and a picture of the plantation where Bass's husband's grandfather lived in slavery. John Silo Bass went on to graduate from medical school and start a line of doctors that continues to the present day.

Freedom Fountain ❸
Liberty, Missouri (east side of the courthouse square)

Historical marker with water fountain. Free. ♿: Yes. Self-guided walking tour available at historicliberty.org.

 Our Take
Spend a moment here while visiting other Liberty sites.

Liberty's African-American community came here nearly 200 years ago as slaves. Local historians have determined that slave auctions were regularly held near the spot of Freedom Fountain. This monument, built in 2000, celebrates the long struggle for freedom and civil rights as well as African-American contributions to the growth and prosperity of Clay County.

Watkins Woolen Mill State Historic Site ❷
★ *A Big Divide Top Site* ★

Lawson, Missouri (26600 Park Road North)

Restored woolen mill, historic home, and state park. Hours: 9:30 to 4:30 Monday thru Saturday, 10:30 to 4:30 Sunday. **Free.** One- and two-hour tours are $4.50 for ages 13+ and $2.50 for ages 6-12. ♿: Visitor center,

A loom from the 1800s, like everything else at Watkins Woolen Mill State Historic Site, looks ready to use.

museum, and first floor of the house. Who runs it: Missouri State Parks (mostateparks.com). Phone: 816-580-3387.

 Our Take

Amazing! A 19th-century woolen mill with original machines intact in a bucolic setting in rural Missouri.

In 1870 there were 2,400 woolen mills operating across the United States. Watkins Woolen Mill is the only surviving mill that still has all of its original machinery, including a 50-horsepower steam boiler that once powered the factory. Stepping inside the three-story, brick structure is like walking into a time warp. Only the skilled workers are missing. Walthus Watkins, the mill's founder, opened for business in 1860. During the Civil War the mill supplied much-needed yarn and cloth to both Union and Confederate clients, but even a woolen mill could not emerge unscathed from the internecine conflict. Near the end of the war Bushwhackers forced Watkins to shut down the mill temporarily. After the war the mill resumed operations. It closed in 1898 — and seemingly no one touched it again until Missouri turned it into a historic site.

Go first to the visitor center to learn more about 19th-century woolen manufacturing and to "meet" the Watkins family and learn about their vision for Bethany Plantation, the community they created for the workers at Watkins Mill. It had worker housing, an octagonal schoolhouse, and a Baptist church. Today the historic site provides sanctuary for rare breeds of sheep and chickens. One-hour tours are available for the Watkins's 12-room home or the mill. A two-hour tour will take you to both. If you've only got an hour, take the mill tour — there's nothing like it in the world.

Watkins Mill is at the center of a beautiful 1,500-acre state park that has 98 mostly electric campsites, a lake, sandy beach, biking/walking paths and equestrian trails.

Town of Kansas Bridge ❻
Kansas City, Missouri (3rd and Main Streets)

Pedestrian bridge and bike route connector in historic location. Free. ♿: Yes. Who maintains it: Port Authority of KC. ✆ 816-559-3750.

 Our Take
Unmatched views of the mighty Missouri River.

The Hannibal Bridge made Kansas City. Built in 1869, it was the first railroad bridge across the Missouri River, turning the bustling town of Kansas overnight into a major rail hub and an urban titan of mid-America. The bridge is long gone, but in its place is the Town of Kansas Bridge, a 650-foot pedestrian walkway to a stunning overlook of the Missouri River. The bridge also provides a bicycle link between the

Town of Kansas Bridge.

city's River Market and its original birthplace on the banks of the Missouri at Riverfront Park. The bike rack on Third Street, added in 2009, conceals a landscaped bioswale that disperses 800 cubic feet of excess storm water from adjacent buildings.

Little House reached its popular peak with Melissa Gilbert's TV portrayal of young Laura Ingalls (left). Visitors still flock to the little house in Missouri (right) where the real Laura wrote the books.

Laura Ingalls Wilder Home and Museum ⓮

Mansfield, Missouri (3068 Highway A, just west of town off Highway 60)

Historic homes and museum. Hours: 9 to 5 Monday thru Saturday, 12:30 to 5 Sunday, March 1 to November 15 only. Admission $10 adults, $8 seniors, $6 ages 6-17. ♿: Yes. Who runs it: The Wilder Association (laurain-gallswilderhome.com). ☎ 877-924-7126.

 Our Take

> This site wonderfully reflects Laura's personality and love of the simple life. Her writing space is intact.

We loved seeing the house where Laura Ingalls Wilder wrote her books. It is simple, eccentric, a little cramped, wonderfully authentic. Wilder was only 4-foot-10, so her husband Almanzo used his woodworking and other handy skills to fashion the kitchen to a woman her height. The Wilders were not attached to modernity, as their house makes clear. It is a charming example of simple, thoughtful living. You'll see the tiny study and desk where Wilder created the books that harken back to a storied time.

The museum was less impressive. A new one is scheduled to be built by 2014, but until then come for the house tours. Don't miss their "other" home, Rocky Ridge, just down the road.

☛ **Local color:** Just outside Mansfield is Bakersville, home to **Baker Creek Heirloom Seeds**, an old-timey pioneer village that serves a delicious lunch daily (2278 Baker Creek Road, ℂ 417-924-8917).

Little House on the Prairie Museum ⓭
near Independence, Kansas (2507 County Road 3000)

Replica cabin with small museum and outbuildings. Hours: 10 to 5 Monday thru Saturday, 1 to 5 Sunday, April to October. Suggested donation $3 adults $1 kids. ♿: Call. Who runs it: privately owned (littlehouseontheprairiemuseum.com). ℂ 620-289-4238.

 Our Take
Little House fans will also enjoy this site.

In 1869 Laura Ingalls Wilder's family left Wisconsin to homestead and eventually arrived on this claim in southeastern Kansas. Like so many other men of that era, Charles Ingalls moved the family around frequently in his quest for greener pastures. In fact, they stayed in Kansas only three years — not enough time to gain title to the land. This site has a replica of the one-room cabin where the Ingalls family lived, along with several outbuildings, surrounded by prairie reminiscent of Laura's time here.

Lanesfield School ⓾
near Edgerton, Kansas (18745 South Dillie Road)

Restored one-room schoolhouse. Hours: 1 to 5 Friday and Saturday or by appointment. **Free.** ♿: Yes. Who runs it: Johnson County Museum. ℂ 913-893-6645.

 Our Take
Best one-room schoolhouse museum we've seen.

Education quickly become a high priority for communities in Kansas after the war. Many counties in Kansas were allocated funds

The one-room schoolhouse at Lanesfield was used for 93 years.

for 100 one-room schools to accommodate all the homesteaders pouring into the state. Most of these schools were eventually abandoned, but Lanesfield School, built in 1869, kept proving itself useful until the 1960s. Johnson County Museum restored it to its appearance in 1904, when it was repaired following a fire.

Lanesfield's appeal is both in its construction and its meticulous renovation. Though one-room schoolhouses made of stone were not uncommon in Kansas, we had never been inside one before. The presence of a knowledgeable guide enhanced our visit. (Be sure to ask to have the school bell rung!) The visitor center has displays on the use of one-room schoolhouses, the role of women in primary education, and a little display on Jim Lane, the school's namesake — though by this point readers of *The Big Divide* may have had enough of him!

Goodnow House State Historic Site ❶
Manhattan, Kansas (2309 Claflin Road)

Historic home. Hours: Tours given 9 to 5 Tuesday to Friday, 2 to 5 weekends. **Free.** ♿: No. Who runs it: Riley County Historical Society, across the parking lot. A Kansas Historic Site (kshs.org). ☏ 785-565-6490.

 Our Take

This historically important 1861 home is notable for the number of original household items still inside.

Isaac and Ellen Goodnow were abolitionist pioneers and educators from Vermont who relocated in Kansas Territory in 1854 and helped establish the free-state town of Manhattan. In 1859 Isaac started a small Methodist college which evolved into Kansas State University, the first land-grant college in the nation. Isaac then became superintendent of Kansas public schools. He is remembered for his insistence on quality education for both sexes.

The Goodnows moved into this two-story stone house in 1861, and the house is furnished in the style of the late 1800s. Because the estate was preserved and handed down among family members, many of the Goodnows' original furnishings and documents survived and are on display, including their dishes, Isaac's writing desk and his extensive personal collections of fossils, minerals, shells, and pottery shards.

☛ **Near here:** Beach Museum of Art (page 86), 1 mile; Flint Hills Discovery Center (page 16), 2 miles

George Washington Carver National Monument ⓯

★ *A Big Divide Top Site* ★

Diamond, Missouri (5646 Carver Road, one-half mile south of Highway V)

Park with visitor center, large museum, nature trail, cemetery, and monument. Hours: 9 to 5 daily; closed New Year's, Thanksgiving, and Christmas days. **Free.** ♿: Visitor center and some walking trails. Who runs it: National Park Service. ℃ 417-325-4151.

 Our Take

Inspirational national park celebrates the life and achievements of a true Renaissance man.

Don't be fooled by the "monument" in the name — this is a full-fledged historic park, with an extensive visitor center/museum

Carver in his Tuskegee Institute laboratory.

and interpretive nature trail, enough to take up a whole morning or afternoon. Most people remember George Washington Carver (1864–1943) as the black scientist who invented 300 uses for the peanut. His ultimate goal, however, was to improve the lives of poor people by promoting self-sufficiency and inexpensive forms of good nutrition.

A professor at Tuskegee Institute in Alabama for many years, Carver realized that Southern soil had become degraded through the monocropping of cotton. He became a strong advocate for the cultivation of peanuts, sweet potatoes, pecans, and soy beans which helped revitalize the soil by putting nutrients back into it. The foods he championed were also particularly healthy food for human consumption.

Carver's accomplishments are all the more remarkable because he was born into slavery and faced widespread racism. When he showed up at a Kansas college that had accepted him (as a museum display tells it), he was barred by school officials who until that moment had no idea he was black.

As we toured this superb national park, we were inspired again and again by Carver's achievements, endless curiosity, and unquenchable optimism.

Gordon Parks:
Pioneering Artist from Kansas

Though he came into the world a half century after George
Washington Carver, Gordon Parks experienced an almost identical
upbringing of poverty and racism along the Missouri-Kansas
border. Like Carver he escaped to friendlier climes and developed
his innate gifts to become a modern Renaissance man. While
Carver thrived in the sciences, Parks excelled in the arts. He was
the first African American to direct a major Hollywood film, first
black staff photographer for *Life* magazine during its heyday, and
an inspiring writer and composer as well.

Parks was the last of 15 children born in 1912 to a tenant farmer
near Fort Scott, Kansas. He attended segregated schools and
learned to watch his step around whites.
After his mother died, Parks was sent to
live with relatives in Minnesota. There he
learned to live off his creative talents, first
with the piano, then with the camera. But
he never really left Kansas. Some of his
best-known work is autobiographical,
like *The Learning Tree,* a bestselling novel
turned into a movie, that draws upon and
redeems his harsh childhood.

Parks in 1963 at the March
on Washington.

In time Fort Scott would recognize him
as a hometown legend. The **Gordon
Parks Museum and Center for Culture
and Diversity** is open weekdays at
Fort Scott Community College (**free;**
2108 S. Horton, © 620-223-2700, ext. 5850) and hosts an annual
celebration of Parks's life. Other photographs and poetry are on
display at **Mercy Hospital** (**free** self-guided tour in the lobby at
401 Woodland Hills Blvd., © 620-223-2200). Parks is buried next
to his parents at **Evergreen Cemetery** on the southern outskirts of
town. A few steps from his gravesite is a large memorial stone with
a poem he composed in 2001 called "Homecoming." It begins: *This
small town into which I was born has, for me, grown into the largest
and most important city in the universe.*

Two restored rail gems: Kansas City's 1914 Union Station (left) and Ottawa's 1888 Old Depot Museum.

Union Station ❼

Kansas City, Missouri (30 West Pershing Road)

Restored train station. Hours: 6 a.m. to midnight daily. **Free;** individual attractions charge fees. ♿: Yes. Who runs it: Union Station (unionstation. org). ✆ 816-460-2020.

Our Take

Worth a trip just to gaze at the ceiling.

Built in 1914, the palatial Union Station was the city's premier transportation center before giving way to the automobile. Its most storied moment was the murder of law enforcement officers outside the terminal on June 17, 1933. The Union Station Massacre was a watershed in the history of the Federal Bureau of Investigation. Soon after, FBI agents were given the authority to carry weapons and make arrests.

Like many rail hubs, Union Station closed in the 1980s, but a decade later voters approved a special sales tax to return it to its 1914 glory. Experts were brought in to determine the exact colors of the original building. Restoration specialists who had worked on Windsor Castle and New York's Grand Central Station patched up the badly damaged ceiling and made it shine again, suspending 12-foot-wide chandeliers weighing 3,500 pounds apiece.

Of the many ways to spend time (and money) inside this magnificent building, we recommend **Science City**, voted one of the top children's science museums by *Parents* magazine; and **Rail Experience,** a museum of railroad history and lore for all ages.

Old Depot Museum ⓫

Ottawa, Kansas (135 West Tecumseh)

Museum. Hours: 9 to 4 Tuesday thru Saturday, 1 to 4 Sunday. Admission: $3 adults, $2 kids 6-17. ♿: Yes. Who runs it: Franklin County Historical Society. ✆ 785-242-1250.

 Our Take

Best county museum in the area.

This restored 1888 Ottawa train depot succeeds at being just as interesting a museum to outsiders as to the locals whose way of life it celebrates. The period rooms here are a step above other county museums, with high-quality interpretive signage and tasteful arranging of artifacts. It's no small thing to make an outsider nostalgic for the local factory or newspaper, as this museum does. You'll also learn here about the novelty publisher whose doctored photos — decades before Photoshop — made Ottawa the postcard capital of the world in the early 1900s.

The first floor has an engaging model train operation, a diorama of a typical Chautauqua from the early 1900s (imagine TED Talks given at a tent city on the prairie), and a cave-like room where you sit in the almost dark and listen to an audio program of "voices" from John Brown's Pottawatomie Creek massacre. Or try to, anyway — when the museum is busy, the voices outside the room are louder than the ones inside. But that is a minor defect in an otherwise exemplary county museum.

Leila's Hair Museum ⓽

Independence, Missouri (1333 South Noland Road)

One-woman museum. Hours: 9 to 4 Tuesday thru Saturday. Admission: $6 ages 13+, $3 seniors and kids. ♿: Yes. Who runs it: Privately operated. ✆ 816-833-2955.

 Our Take

Unique, fascinating collection of Victorian hair art.

From the time she opened her cosmetology school more than 40 years ago, Leila Cohoon has collected wreaths, jewelry, framed art, and religious items — all made from human hair. She claims to have the largest collection of hair art in the world, and after a visit to her museum we will not question that assertion. Most of her collection — more than 150 wreaths and hundreds of other pieces — date to the Victorian era in the late 1800s, the heyday of this at times exquisite art form. It was a time when people remembered and memorialized their loved ones after death, using snippets of their locks in brooches and bracelets or creating elaborate wreaths from the combined hair of a family or fraternal organization.

Cohoon knows the provenance of most of the items in her small museum, where every foot of wall and counter space is filled with the fruits of her relentless collecting. The museum could profit from thematic or chronological grouping and some professional interpretation. Still, it is quite a window into a more sentimental age than our own and a reminder that though humanity has shared many traits throughout the ages, the expression of culture is unique in every era in ways that are sometimes hard to explain.

Outdoor Living History Sites

 Our Take

Nice ways to spend an hour or an afternoon, especially if you have kids with energetic legs.

Old Jefferson Town ➎

Oskaloosa, Kansas (703 Walnut Street). Buildings open weekend afternoons May to September. **Free.** ♿: Call. Info: Contact LeAnn Chapman of the Jefferson County Historical Society, ✆ 785–863–3257.

You can walk down the wooden sidewalk of Old Jefferson Town, set in 1880, visiting the shops, taking a pleasant walk across the brook to tour a fully furnished Victorian home, or the school and chapel buildings. This site includes the childhood home of artist John Steuart Curry (page 86) and a distinctive wind-wagon sculpture.

Shoal Creek Living History Museum ❽

Kansas City, Missouri (7000 NE Barry Road). Open dawn to dusk. **Free.** ⓺: Gravelly. Who runs it: KC Parks and Rec. ☏ 816-792-2655.

Shoal Creek has seventeen original structures built between 1807 and 1885, ranging from a simple pioneer cabin to an antebellum brick mansion. The site covers 80 acres of lovely rolling country in northeast Kansas City — lots of spaces for running, playing, and picnicking. The museum holds classes in handicrafts like tatting and sponsors a fall festival in October among other events. Check the website before going.

Mound City Historical Park ⓬

Mound City, Kansas (700 Main Street). Open dawn to dusk year-round. **Free.** ⓺: No. Info: Call Skip Childress. ☏ 913-795-2074.

This park is less of an old-timey village so much as an eclectic collection of buildings of historical significance to the town. They include a reproduction of Jayhawker James Montgomery's cabin and the 1886 train depot. Mound City is on our scenic Highway 52 driving tour (page 131).

This turn-of-the-20th-century persimmon log cabin, considered the last of its kind, is restored and sits in Mound City Historical Park.

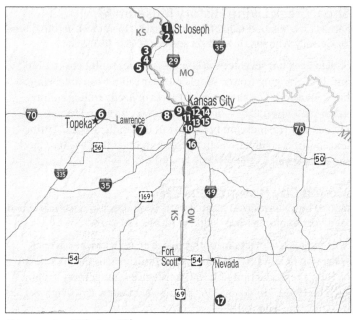

Sites in This Chapter

Tip: The Orientation Map on page 248 shows all Big Divide towns.

School segregation protest in St. Louis, circa 1954.

≈≈≈ 9 ≈≈≈

Liberty and Justice for All

Touring the Missouri-Kansas border region, a visitor could spend weeks immersed in the 19th century. But The Big Divide also has several first-class destinations of more recent vintage. We call these the "liberty and justice" sites as a way of thinking about the dual dramas that consumed the nation for much of the 20th century — defending liberty abroad and fighting for justice at home.

Few actors were more consequential in these dramas than the man from Independence, Harry S. Truman, our thirty-third president. In the service of liberty, Truman served in World War I, brought an end to World War II, started the Korean War, ordered the Berlin Airlift, and formed NATO. In the pursuit of justice, he called the first federal civil rights commission, desegregated the armed forces, and split the Democratic Party in 1948 over civil rights, resulting in the election of his opponent, Thomas E. Dewey ... *not!*

The Oval Office exhibit at the **Harry S. Truman Presidential Library and Museum** (page 205) is organized around these and other decisions of destiny. No 20th-century president would have to make so many choices of such magnitude — except of course for Franklin D. Roosevelt, and he was the act Truman had to follow.

F. D. R. was a patrician who formed a bond with the common man. Truman *was* the common man. The $685 house of his birth could not have been more modest if it had been a log cabin (**Truman Birthplace State Historic Site,** page 207). Truman was the last president not to earn a college degree, having dropped out in order to help his father on the **Truman Farm** (page 209). Instead, he educated himself through reading, a lifelong passion that was instilled by his mother. His love of history started with a set of books she gave him as a boy, all about the generals and battles of the Civil War.

"My debt to history is one which cannot be calculated," Truman once said. Indeed, two of the most important decisions of Truman's presidency were informed by the Civil War. In deciding what to do with his popular but insubordinate general, Douglas MacArthur, Truman drew on the example of Abraham Lincoln relieving command from his popular but insubordinate general, George B. McClellan. And historian Ethan Rafuse has noted that Truman's decision to spend billions helping Europe rebuild after World War II was also rooted in Civil War history. Growing up, Harry had heard all

The recently opened Noland Home, across the street from the Truman Home, offers more glimpses into Bess and Harry's life together.

the stories about his relatives being harassed by Jim Lane's "Red Legs" for the crime of living along the Missouri border. Federal troops tortured his uncle and namesake, Harrison Young, and his family suffered terribly under Order No. 11. These actions created such bitterness that decades later, when Truman's mother visited the White House, she refused to sleep in the Lincoln Bedroom. The lesson was clear. "You can't be vindictive after a war," said Truman.

After the presidency, he continued to read avidly. His unending interest in the great conflict led him to start Kansas City's Civil War Roundtable. He supervised the creation of his presidential library, choosing the great Thomas Hart Benton to paint the entry lobby (**Thomas Hart Benton State Historic Site**, page 206). Most nights, Harry and Bess would be in their cozy reading room at 219 North Delaware Street, now the **Truman Home** (page 207), where his books of history and biography are still on the shelves, squeezed by the mysteries that Bess loved.

We think Harry would have enjoyed the **National World War I Museum at Liberty Memorial** (page 210), which was commissioned by Congress in 2004 and opened two years later. He would have commented favorably on the aisles of displays, timelines, and multimedia, all very much up to a history buff's demanding standards. The museum's tone is relentlessly grim, but then it was a grim war, and Truman was not one to extol the glories of combat.

While not as spit-and-polish as the World War I Museum, the collection of artifacts inside St. Joseph's teeming **National Military Heritage Museum** (page 211) serves as a counterpoint to the other's gloom and doom. Hand-crafted over more than two decades by devoted volunteers, this warehouse of memorabilia reflects a more upbeat view of the military's role in preserving American freedoms abroad.

But the definition of freedom itself has been in constant expansion since the Civil War broke the chains of bondage for four million Americans. Three important museums added in the past 15 years show that full equality for black Americans would involve a long struggle.

The most richly interpreted of these is Topeka's **Brown v. Board of Education National Historic Site** (page 211). It tells the story of the Supreme Court's 1954 decision ending legally-mandated school segregation. In the process it tells how African Americans were forced into second-class citizenship for more than 80 years after the Civil War and how *Brown v. Board* did not bring an end to racial discrimination so much as launch a new era in the quest for equality and opportunity.

The **Negro Leagues Baseball Museum** and **American Jazz Museum** (page 213) and associated music venues (**Blue Room and Gem Theater**, page 214) function, in a way, as backdoor civil-rights museums. They celebrate a time when African Americans were expected to create their own culture

One of Hollywood's classic musical numbers, "The Atchison, Topeka and the Santa Fe," from *The Harvey Girls* (1947), plays at Atchison County Historical Museum (page 217) with a film about the town's rail history.

— and did such a good job of it that the white mainstream could not help but pay attention.

It's common for visitors to the Negro Leagues Museum to wonder how major league baseball would have been different had Negro League greats like Josh Gibson and Satchel Paige been allowed to play in their primes. Likewise, we have wondered how different this town we call home would be today had its black citizens been allowed to live the way that Charlie Parker and Count Basie played — that is, anywhere they liked. The **Johnson County Museum** (page 222) is notable for its exhibit on the pox of racial segregation in suburban housing. Eventually these practices ended, and even the cemeteries were integrated. At Kansas City's **Forest Hill Cemetery,** two local civil-rights heroes are buried just a few feet away from the area's best-loved slaveholding Confederate general (page 214).

At Haskell Indian Nations University in Lawrence, Kansas, **Haskell Cultural Center and Museum** (page 215) continues a narrative that begins with the sites in Chapter 2, "First People." Here, the stories of Haskell students are used to narrate the story of white efforts to make Indians conform to mainstream culture and the cultural-identity movement that developed and pushed back against it.

We wish we had come upon a women's rights museum that measured up to the standard set by the Brown v. Board and Haskell sites. But at least we have Amelia. Each year thousands of visitors come to Atchison, Kansas, to walk through the house where in 1897 the most beloved aviator of all time was born. The **Amelia Earhart Birthplace Museum** (page 218) is a collection of Earhart memorabilia, from childhood to the peak of her celebrity, inside a beautifully restored home overlooking the Missouri River. We recommend starting at the **Atchison County Museum** (page 217) to get a fuller picture of Earhart's upbringing and career.

The **Glore Psychiatric Museum** in St. Joseph (page 219) is listed in *Weird Missouri* and other travel guides, which never fail to note that the Glore is one of America's strangest museums. Composed of artifacts from the former State Hospital No. 2, it tells the history of that institution and the evolution of care for mental illness. While there is no denying the oddball factor of the Glore, its creator — a longtime member of the state hospital's staff — meant for his exhibits to convey the dignity and humanity of the mentally ill and to remind the world of how they were once treated. In our opinion, they do just that.

Finally, it seems appropriate to close this guide by inviting you to see history being made first-hand. Every month or so, the U.S. District Court in Kansas holds naturalization ceremonies on the sixth floor of the Robert J. Dole Courthouse in downtown Kansas City, Kansas. Outside the courtroom is a superb new exhibit, **Americans by Choice** (page 221), featuring some of the thousands of stories of people who have taken the naturalization oath here. As their first act of citizenship, these new Americans face the flag and pledge allegiance to that nation for which it stands — once divided, now indivisible — "with liberty and justice for all."

Harry Truman (at left in entryway) and Thomas Hart Benton stand beneath Benton's mural at the Truman Presidential Library and Museum, circa 1961.

Truman Presidential Library & Museum ⓯

Independence, Missouri (500 West Highway 24; exit I-70 at Noland Road)

★ A Big Divide Top Site ★

Large museum with research library. Hours: 9 to 5 daily, 1 to 5 Sunday. Open until 9 on Thursdays in summer. Admission $8 adults, $7 seniors, $3 youth ages 5+. ♿: Yes. Who runs it: National Archives (trumanlibrary.org). ✆ 816-268-8200.

Our Take

Marvel at all Harry had on his plate as President. Admire the qualities that made him a successful politician.

We recommend a full day, if you can spare it, to tour this expertly curated, fair-minded presidential museum and the Harry S. Truman National Historic Site (page 207), with breaks.

Your museum visit begins with one or both of the introductory films. The longer one is about 45 minutes. While waiting for that to start, spend some time studying the lobby mural, *Independence and the Opening of the West,* by Thomas Hart Benton, whose Kansas City home is also a historic site (page 206). It isn't as daring as the earlier Bentons on display at the Nelson-Atkins Museum (page 44). But it does tell quite a story, and Truman — who had chosen Benton to paint it and became friends with him during the project — declared the mural to be the artist's "finest work."

Two major galleries dominate the museum. "Harry S. Truman: His Life and Times," opened in 2004, uses the voluminous

Liberty and Justice for All   **205**

correspondence between Harry and Bess to narrate his ascent from dirt farmer to World War I captain to county politician to the U.S. Senate and then the White House. After you've had a break (or gone on a house tour), head back to the museum, watch the shorter film, then step into the new, 10,500-square-foot gallery on Truman's presidency.

Setbacks aren't overlooked here — Truman never did get a universal health care bill through Congress, and Korea was a mess. The exhibits make clear that he governed with a strong moral compass and common sense but could also be peevish, hot-tempered, and stubborn, qualities that spill out in his private correspondence and the occasional angry memo. Truman claimed never to have lost sleep over his decision to drop the atomic bomb on Japan. But Korea vexed him greatly, as you will learn by reading a poignant letter from a grieving parent — especially when you hear where a museum curator found it.

Before leaving, step into the courtyard and pay your respects to Harry, Bess, Margaret, and Margaret's husband Clifton Daniel, all buried here.

Thomas Hart Benton State Historic Site ⑩

Kansas City, Missouri (3616 Belleview; bus tours should call ahead for directions that avoid neighborhood traffic circles)

Historic home and studio. Hours: 10 to 4 Monday and Thursday-Saturday, noon to 4 Sunday. Tours $4 adults. ♿: Call. Who runs it: State of Missouri (mostateparks.com). ☎ 816-931-5722.

 Our Take

Charming home gives insights into Benton's life.

Thomas Hart Benton and his wife Rita Benton were in this Arts and Crafts house nearly 40 years, and Missouri has preserved it much as it was when Rita died, 11 weeks after Tom did, just as he was about to sign a mural in his studio in 1975.

The tour acquaints you with the Bentons and their life here. Though Tom became a famous artist in his lifetime, this comfortable but unpretentious house bears witness to Rita's financial acumen and frugality that got them through the lean years. Nearby, the Nelson-Atkins Museum of Art (page 44) has 18 Bentons currently on display. If you're in or near Jefferson City, see Benton's acclaimed mural series, *A Social History of the State of Missouri,* at the Missouri State Capitol (reservations recommended; ℂ 573-751-2854). And of course, don't miss the Benton mural at the Truman Library (see photo, page 205).

Truman Birthplace State Historic Site ⑱
Lamar, Missouri (1009 Truman)

Historic home. Hours: 10 to 4 Wednesday thru Saturday and noon to 4 Sunday, except in winter. **Free.** ♿: Visitor center and first floor of house. Who runs it: the state of Missouri (mostateparks.com). ℂ 417-682-2279 (also Battle of Carthage tours).

 Our Take
Small home has a modest story to tell.

Harry Truman had as humble a beginning as any modern U.S. president. His father, John Truman, was farming and working as a livestock dealer when he paid $15 for a doctor to come to this little white-framed house on May 8, 1884, and deliver the family's firstborn child. The home has no family artifacts now but is furnished in a style reminiscent of the 1880s. Two monuments in the yard, including one by the American Legion, pay tribute to the future president. Short guided tours are the only way to access the house. The visitor center across the street has a gift shop with books and old-fashioned toys. It's a long way from Independence, but Lamar is right off I-49 (Highway 71) en route to the Civil War battlefields further south.

Harry S. Truman Visitor Center, Truman Home, and the Noland Home ⑯
Independence, Missouri (223 North Main St., off Independence Square)

Historic home museums, plus downtown visitor center. Hours: 8:30 to 5 Tuesday thru Sunday, daily during the summer. Tours are $4 for visitors ages 15+. ♿: Yes. Who runs it: National Park Service (nps.gov/hstr). ℂ 816-254-2720.

A view from inside the iron gate the Secret Service erected in 1949 to keep tourists away from the Truman home in Independence, Mo. "Never did like it and never will like it," Harry once said of the fence.

💬 Our Take

An authentic look into the former President's private life. The Noland Home is a welcome new addition.

At last, the truth can be told: Harry and Bess Truman were pack rats! Over 58,000 historical artifacts were found in the Trumans' home on North Delaware Street in Independence after Bess died in 1982. Many were gifts from the Trumans' years in Washington, but most of what you'll see on your house tour was theirs. They just hung onto things.

That's one of the charming discoveries you'll make on your tour, which you must reserve in person at the Visitor Center on Independence Square. While there, you can watch a narrated slide show, about 12 minutes long, about the Truman family. Consider booking your tour several hours in advance and spending the rest of your day at the **Harry S. Truman Presidential Library and Museum** (page 205). Here's a tip: Download all the brochures from the park service's website (see above) to brush up before your visit.

When your tour group assembles at the house on Delaware, you'll enter through the back — and immediately be struck by the cozy, some might say cramped, kitchen where Bess preferred to have breakfast in the years after Harry died. The linoleum is worn and even patched in one place. The rest of the house is large and well-appointed, but not nearly as fancy as one might expect from the former First Couple. The den is where the Trumans spent many nights listening to records and reading books, and looks it. Harry's and Bess's coats still hang in a vestibule.

After your tour walk across Delaware Street and into the Noland Home. This is where Harry's cousins Nellie and Ethel Noland invited him to meet their neighbor Bess Wallace for the first time. Their freshly renovated home is a new addition to the historic site, with a gallery that takes you deeper into the Trumans' domestic life. Family photos, sound recordings of private occasions, revealing correspondence — Margaret Truman called her father "a demon letter-writer" — and a video from the 1950s of Margaret interviewing Harry and Bess on CBS are all here.

Truman Farm ⑰
Grandview, Missouri (12301 Blue Ridge Boulevard)

Farmhouse and outbuildings. Hours: See below. **Free.** ♿: Yes. Who runs it: National Park Service. Info: Call Truman National Historic Site. ℂ 816-254-9929.

 Our Take
Useful to understanding the young Truman's hard life.

Hard times forced Harry to quit school and return here to the family's Grandview farm, where he would spend eleven long years doing work he did not particularly enjoy. Reflecting on that period of his life, he said that being out with a horse-drawn plow gave him a lot of time to read and think. Harry slept in an unheated room upstairs with the hired hands. The rest of the Truman clan was also on the farm — his grandmother, mother, father (who died in 1914), brother, and sister. He finally escaped when he memorized the vision test and got himself inducted into the Army in 1917.

☛ **No more tours:** As this book went to press, the National Park Service was uncertain whether it would be able to staff this site for weekend tours in 2013. Call ahead to check. The farm is always open for visitors to walk around the buildings and read the interpretive signage, which is quite good. There's also a cell-phone tour (✆ 585-672-2611).

National World War I Museum ⓫

Kansas City, Missouri (100 West 26th Street, across from Union Station)

★ A Big Divide Top Site ★

Museum and Liberty Memorial tower. Hours: 10 to 5 Tuesday thru Sunday, 10 to 5 daily during the summer. Two-day admission is $14 for adults, $12 seniors and students, $8 ages 6+. ♿: Museum yes, tower no. Who runs it: private foundation (theworldwar.org). ✆ 816-784-1918.

 Our Take

This first-rate, freshly interpreted museum casts a dark pall over the "war to end all wars."

World War I is largely remembered today as a cautionary war, from its origins in hubris and bloodlust to its vindictive Armistice, which sowed the seeds for the next war two decades later. This outstanding museum, authorized in 2004 by Congress, presents a solemn and unflinching look at the Great War that is true to that public memory.

Like other big museums, it uses state-of-the-art techniques to provide an immersive experience, whether introducing visitors to the players and politics of prewar Europe and America, or parachuting visitors into the thick of combat with theatrics like a scale-model bunker and dramatic eyewitness accounts of the grim trench warfare that stretched on for months without resolution.

Other exhibits include wall-length timelines, the role of World War I in art and culture, the entry of America into the war, and the usual truckloads of equipment and artifacts from the battle front and home front. Your two-day ticket includes a ride to the top of the Liberty Memorial, dedicated in 1927 and offering a 360-degree view of Kansas City, plus admission to the temporary exhibits in the two buildings flanking the memorial. Other museum amenities include an audio tour (rental), café, and gift shop.

National Military Heritage Museum ❷

St. Joseph, Missouri (701 Messanie Street)

Large museum. Hours: 9 to 5 daily, 9 to 1 Saturday. **Free.** ♿: Call. Privately operated (nationalmilitaryheritagemuseum.com). ☏ 816-233-4321.

 Our Take

Big collection of military paraphernalia is impressive but lacks professional interpretation.

This four-building repository of 20,000 military artifacts was the brainchild of a retired 28-year Army veteran, Franklin Flesher, who was at his desk poring over donations on the day we toured the site. The main building, an 1890 Romanesque brick palace, contains battle murals, uniform displays, dioramas, a replica World War I trench from a movie set, model airplanes and ships, *Lego* model submarines and carriers, combat medals, marching-band instruments, displays on the Santa Fe Trail, Lewis and Clark, the Civil War, and on and on. The missing ingredient is interpretation. How are we to think about all these implements of destruction and patriotic gear? What does it mean in terms of our nation's freedom?

A volunteer is usually available for guided tours. Ask to visit the garage where the jeeps, ambulances, two-and-a-half ton military truck, Huey and Cobra helicopters, and other vehicles are kept.

Brown v. Board of Education National Historic Site ❻

Topeka, Kansas (1515 SE Monroe Street)

★ *A Big Divide Top Site* ★

Museum inside historic site. Hours: 9 to 5 daily. **Free.** ♿: Yes. Who runs it: National Park Service (nps.gov/brvb). ☏ 785-354-4273.

 Our Take

The school at the center of the Supreme Court's 1954 segregation case is now a premier civil rights museum.

The Wyandotte Constitution brought Kansas into the Union as a free state but did not prevent school districts from practicing racial

The opening game of the 1924 Negro Leagues World Series, played in Kansas City. George Sweatt, the Kansas City Monarchs great (standing next to team owner J.L. Wilkinson, leftmost man in hat), is honored at the Humboldt Historical Museum in his hometown (page 121).

segregation. Nearly one century later, that flawed vision of equality was corrected — at least on paper — by the Supreme Court of the United States.

Brown v. Board of Education was actually five separate school segregation cases consolidated, with Topeka's Monroe Elementary at the heart of the matter. This school, after its closing, was chosen as home for one of the nation's premier civil rights museums.

Topeka's high schools and middle schools had long been integrated, and no sentiment stronger than tradition kept its elementary schools segregated. But that tradition was legal, thanks to the Supreme Court's 1896 ruling in *Plessy v. Ferguson* allowing "separate but equal" institutions for the races. Civil rights leaders argued that separate had never meant equal. In one of the plaintiff's other school districts, Clarendon County, South Carolina, the board of education was spending four times as much money on white schools as on black ones.

Start your visit in the theater and watch all the segments in the multi-screen video production. Through a simple series of dramatized conversations between a curious teenager and her grandfather, you'll understand where *Brown v. Board* fits into the larger sweep of civil rights history. Two large galleries and a book lovers' gift shop make up the rest of the site. The galleries are dense with information, and while the signs are generally concise, there are a lot of them to see and read.

The site's most unique exhibit is the "Hall of Courage," which simulates the experience of black students entering an all-white school while running a gauntlet of taunting, jeering bystanders. Elsewhere, a series of videos shows schoolkids taking conflicting positions on racial issues. It's a good reminder that the pursuit of justice is never as easy as it looks, especially in hindsight.

Negro Leagues Baseball Museum and American Jazz Museum ⑫
Kansas City, Missouri (1616 East 18th Street, near Vine)

Museum complex. Open 9 to 6 Tuesday thru Saturday, noon to 6 Sunday. Admission: $10 adults for one museum, $15 combo ticket. Discounts for seniors and children, kids under 5 free. &: Yes. Who runs it: private foundation (nlbm.com and americanjazzmuseum.com). ℂ 816-221-1920.

 Our Take
These stylish twin museums celebrate the achievements of African Americans in an age of segregation.

This is a shrine to an era that didn't have to happen. The Negro Leagues of baseball (1920-1955) were the response to Jim Crow and racism that kept black players out of the majors. The first Negro League was organized in Kansas City and the game's most successful franchise was based here too — the Monarchs of Satchel Paige, George Sweatt, Cool Papa Bell, and other greats. The Negro Leagues museum highlights these and many other ballplayers and tells the story of the various black baseball's leagues whose fortunes rose and fell with the sport's perilous economics. Finally, it explains how civil rights progress helped put the Negro Leagues out of business.

Next door, the American Jazz Museum features the work of four of jazz's most innovative and influential musicians: Louis Armstrong, Duke Ellington, Ella Fitzgerald, and Kansas City's own Charlie Parker. This is an interactive museum, with listening stations and videos, even a recording studio that encourages visitors to experiment with making their own music.

☛ **Local flavor:** For the complete Kansas City experience, visit one of the iconic barbecue joints near the museums: Arthur Bryant's, just east at 18th and Brooklyn, or Gates at 12th and Brooklyn.

The Blue Room and Gem Theater ⓭

Kansas City, Missouri (both are adjacent to the above museum complex)

Nightclub/theater. The Blue Room is open four nights a week, the Gem for special events. ♿: Yes. Both are affiliated with the American Jazz Museum. ℂ 816-474-8463 and 816-474-6262.

 Our Take

It's a museum — and a jazz venue (our favorite, in fact).

The Blue Room, which is attached to the American Jazz Museum and is considered its performance arm, was rated one of the top jazz clubs in the world in 2012 by *DownBeat* magazine. The venue is intimate, the sound superb, and all the cocktail tables are museum displays. It is a smoke-free club and has been since it opened in 1997.

The restored Gem Theater plays host to the "Jammin' at the Gem" series featuring international jazz artists, and an annual gospel concert in honor of the Negro Leagues Baseball Museum's longtime ambassador, the late Buck O'Neil.

☛ **Local sound:** The best place to learn what's playing around town is JAM, the Jazz Ambassadors Magazine (kcjazzambassadors.com).

Forest Hill Cemetery ⓮

Kansas City, Missouri (6901 Troost)

Open dawn to dusk. Free. ℂ 816-523-2114.

One of the most beloved Confederate soldiers in the West, Gen.

Joseph O. "Jo" Shelby, is buried in Kansas City, surrounded by other rebel graves at a magnificent pillar in the southeast corner of Forest Hill Cemetery. But the old rebel has some very surprising neighbors these days — two African-American men who made civil rights history. You can't miss the gravesite memorial for Satchel Paige, the greatest pitcher of the Negro Leagues and baseball Hall of Famer, since it is steps away from Shelby's memorial. And on your way to those graves is the small tombstone for Steven L. Harvey, a popular Kansas City musician who was murdered in 1981. When Harvey's killer walked free in district court for lack of proof, the Justice Department stepped in and gathered enough

Top to bottom: Gravestones for Jo Shelby, Satchel Paige, and Steven Harvey.

evidence to secure a conviction and life sentence on the charge that the suspect had violated his victim's civil rights. This novel tactic of re-prosecuting hate crimes would be used again 11 years later in the Rodney King case and inspire new efforts to solve many civil rights cold cases.

Haskell Cultural Center and Museum ❼
Lawrence, Kansas (155 Indian Avenue, 1 block south of 23rd and Barker)

Museum. Hours: 10 to 5 weekdays, closed for lunch. **Free admission** but donations suggested. ♿: Yes. Who runs it: Haskell Indian Nations University (haskell.edu). ☏ 785-832-6686.

 Our Take
Small, inspiring museum covers history of Haskell Indian Nations University and Indian identity politics.

At the time Haskell was established as an Indian boarding school in 1884, the federal government's assimilationist policy required students to stay at the institution for four years. They were

Haskell Institute students, Lawrence, Kansas, 1908.

forbidden any contact with their families; many students died and were buried here without their parents being notified. Today, Haskell Indian Nations University is a four-year university with students from all nationally recognized Indian tribes. How it got from there to here is the focus of this museum.

The permanent exhibit, "Honoring Our Children Through Seasons of Sacrifice, Survival, Change, and Celebration," divides the history of Haskell into four sections, which parallel trends in American Indian identity politics. Ultimately the students pushed back against efforts to bury their national identities, and their activism probably saved Haskell, now a place where Indian heritage is studied and celebrated.

The cultural center also has a trove of photographs, documents, and artifacts such as headdresses, bead work, and pottery that may be on display. A large medicine wheel on the floor is a symbol of healing, as is the medicinal garden outside. The Peace Pole, a gift from Japanese donors, has its message of peace written in English, Navajo, Japanese, and Cherokee. There is a self-guided tour available at the front desk, but we recommend a guided tour (schedule at least a week in advance).

Atchison County Historical Society ❹
Atchison, Kansas (200 South 10th Street)

County museum located in historic depot. Hours: 9 to 5 Monday thru Saturday, noon to 5 Sunday, shorter hours in the off-season. **Free.** ♿: Yes. Who runs it: Atchison Chamber of Commerce (atchisonkansas. net). ☎ 913-367-6238.

 Our Take
Useful display on Amelia Earhart's life.

Before you go to the Amelia Earhart Birthplace Museum (see below), we suggest that you stop at this combination visitor center and historical museum located in a restored railroad freight depot. The Earhart exhibit is modest but gives a chronology of her life and other details you won't find at the birthplace site. You can also see the fabulous evening dress she wore during her triumphal return to Kansas. The other notable exhibit in this county museum is a railroad theater showing a documentary on the history of Atchison rails and a clip from the 1946 film *The Harvey Girls* featuring Judy Garland and a cast of dozens performing "On the Atchison, Topeka, and the Santa Fe."

☛ **Rail Museum (free):** Outside the building is Atchison's Outdoor Rail Museum, owned by a volunteer group of local railroad enthusiasts. There are about two dozen gritty rail cars here of different vintages. You can visit the site year-round but on summer weekends the cars are open for walkthroughs. Call ahead to the number above.

Amelia Earhart knew how to combine high flying with high fashion.

Amelia Earhart Birthplace Museum ❸
Atchison, Kansas (223 North Terrace Street)

Historic home with exhibits. Hours: 9 to 4 weekdays, 10 to 4 Saturday, 1 to 4 Sunday. Admission $4 adults, $1 children 12 and under. ♿: First floor. Privately operated (ameliaearhartmuseum.org). ✆ 913-367-4217.

 Our Take

Restored home does bring you up-close and personal with the famed aviator. Lacks a guided tour.

The Ninety-Nines, an international group of women pilots that Amelia Earhart helped found, bought the birthplace house of Earhart in 1984 and spent 13 years restoring it to its turn-of-the-century appearance. The restoration work won an award from the Kansas Historical Society and is indeed first-rate.

There is not much signage or interpretation, however, other than a self-guided tour brochure you're given upon paying your entry fee. We'd like to see a more professional presentation to the exhibits and more attention paid to her aviation exploits. Earhart was not only the second person to complete a trans-Atlantic flight but the first to fly from Hawaii to the U.S. mainland.

Still, there is no denying this is a historically significant house with plenty to look at. Artifacts throughout the house include media mentions of Earhart's exploits, as well as her career as a magazine writer, her marriage to publishing magnate George P. Putnam, and the couple's business ventures, such as the AE clothing line, "for the woman who likes to live actively." A display (in the kitchen, of all places) examines theories about her disappearance on a round-the-world flight in 1937. It's this mystery, as much as anything, that helps keep the legend of Amelia Earhart going strong.

☞ **Local color:** Every July Atchison holds an Amelia Earhart Festival. Check the museum's website for information.

☞ **Amelia Earhart Earthworks:** Renowned Kansas artist Stan Herd created a one-acre landscape showing Amelia in flying gear. Located just outside town near the International Forest of Friendship on the south end of town off Highway 73. Info and directions: 800-234-1854.

Glore Psychiatric Museum ❶
St. Joseph, Missouri (3406 Frederick Avenue)

★ A Big Divide Top Site ★

Museum on historic site. Hours: 10 to 5 Monday thru Saturday, 1 to 5 Sunday. Admission $5 adults, $4 seniors, $3 students; ticket gains entry to all three of the St. Joseph Museums. ♿: Yes. Who runs it: St. Joseph Museums (stjosephmuseum.org). ℂ 816-232-8471.

 Our Take
Thought-provoking, unsettling look at treatment of the mentally ill. **Not recommended for young children**.

George Glore worked for the Missouri Department of Mental Health for 41 years, and most of those years he was a man with a mission — to build this museum. We're hard pressed to think of any place that recreates a bygone era so viscerally as the Glore does in transporting its visitors back to the institutional era of mid-20th-century mental health care.

The St. Joseph Museums, including the Glore, are in a building complex that originally housed State Hospital No. 2. Many patients were permanently institutionalized here. At one point the hospital had its own self-sufficient farm operation, machine shop, and other industries all displayed here in minimalist settings.

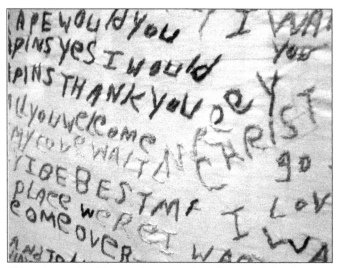

This poignant jumble — today we might call it a word cloud — was embroidered by a patient with schizophrenia at the State Hospital in St. Joseph, now the Glore Psychiatric Museum.

A row of rocking chairs shows where less capable patients were expected to while away the hours and not bother the staff. Patients with more extreme problems received more extreme measures: forced ice baths, isolation chambers, electroshock and, yes, brain manipulation.

The remarkable thing about the Glore is that the exhibits are presented so well that one can empathize with both the poor patients and their poor caregivers — who were, after all, urged to treat patients as if they were their own children. Over the years the more barbaric treatments would be replaced with occupational therapy and other practices that acknowledged the dignity of the patient. Those chapters are represented here with rooms dedicated to practical arts like sewing, jewelry-making, and car restoration.

And there is the bizarro side of the Glore, the aspect that gets it written up in other travel guides. We can't deny that we, too, were riveted by the oddball pieces of unintended performance art, like the 108,000 cigarette packs collected by a patient who was convinced he could redeem them for a wheelchair, or the needlepoint ramblings of a patient that filled up a bedsheet, or the eerily beautiful arrangement of 1,446 objects found in the stomach of a patient whose swallowing obsession proved fatal.

Your tour ends in a room of horrors — full-sized replicas of devices used in previous centuries to treat the mentally ill through bloodletting, lockup, or near-drowning experiences (sometimes minus the "near"). The replicas were built by patients under the direction of George Glore to dramatize the progress society has made in caring for the mentally ill.

Americans by Choice ❾

Kansas City, Kansas (Robert J. Dole U.S. Courthouse, 500 State Avenue)

Exhibit. Hours: 8 to 5 weekdays. Free street parking on 6th and State, or use nearby public garage. **Free.** ♿: Yes. See security note below. Operated by U.S. District Court of Kansas (ksd.uscourts.gov). ℭ 913-735-2205.

💬 Our Take

Inspiring exhibit shows why and how immigrants qualify to become naturalized U.S. citizens.

In the years following the Civil War, Kansas had the highest rate of immigration in the nation, much of it from abroad. Today, some 2,400 individuals become naturalized U.S. citizens in Kansas every year, including hundreds on the sixth floor of the U.S. District Courthouse.

It is there you will find "Americans by Choice," a well-done permanent exhibit on the history of immigration with a focus on Kansas past and present. Photographs, documents, maps, and a video produced with recently-arrived area immigrants bring the subject to life. There's even a sample citizenship exam

Outdoor naturalization ceremonies like this one are a community occasion at Fort Scott, Kansas.

you can take. (Quick, which U.S. president helped write the Federalist Papers — Adams, Jefferson, or Madison?)

The Kansas Naturalization website lists the dates of upcoming ceremonies for inducting new U.S. citizens. Or call the phone number above. We recommend combining a visit to the exhibit on one of those days. Arrive at least 30 minutes before the ceremony, as the courtroom fills up quickly.

☛ **Security check:** You'll need a valid photo ID to enter the courthouse. Leave your phone, camera, and other electronic devices in the trunk of your car — they won't make it past the grumpy security guards. Cameras are permitted during naturalization ceremonies.

☛ **Outdoor ceremony:** Fort Scott National Historic Site (page 40) hosts an outdoors naturalization ceremony in the fall. It's a festive occasion and hundreds from town turn out for it.

Local Museum Spotlight

Johnson County Museum ❽
Shawnee, Kansas (6305 Lackman Road). Open 10 to 4:30 Monday thru Saturday. **Free.** Tours of All-Electric home are $2 adults, $1 kids. ♿: Yes. Operated by Johnson County (jocomuseum.org). ✆ 913-715-2550.

The museum's two best features are its outstanding play area for children — a town of pint-sized storefronts, including doctor's office, theater, and golf course — and the 1954 All-Electric Home, a model home built by the local utility to showcase modern design (open only for afternoon tours). Johnson County, Kansas, was a classic postwar suburban mecca. Between 1940 and 1950 the county's population doubled in size, and doubled again between 1950 and 1960. You'll learn here how the U.S. government facilitated the growth of the suburbs by making home ownership affordable to many people. But you'll also learn that it took the Fair Housing movement to extend this generosity to all races and religious groups.

Extras

Visitor Centers

The VCs below have a wide selection of brochures and maps and are excellent resources for finding motels and restaurants. Some publish visitor guides for ordering or download. Like many of the sites in this book, VCs often reduce their hours in the off-season (November to March).

Atchison Visitor Center, Atchison, KS (700 S. 10th, in the restored 1880s Santa Fe freight depot). Open 8 to 6 daily May 15 to September 15 and 9 to 5 daily rest of year. Website atchisonkansas.net. ℂ 913-367-2427.

Baxter Springs Route 66 Visitor Center, Baxter Springs, KS (Military Avenue at 10th Street). Open 10 to 4 daily, but call ahead (site is staffed by volunteers). Housed in the restored 1930 Independent Oil and Gas Service Station. Website: baxterspringsmuseum.org. ℂ 620-856-2066.

Carthage Visitors Bureau, Carthage, MO (402 S. Garrison Ave.). Open 8:30 to 5 weekdays. Website: visitcarthage.com.

Fort Scott Visitor Center, Fort Scott, KS (231 Wall). Open 8 to 5 weekdays, 10 to 4 Saturday. Website: fortscott.com. ℂ 620-223-3574.

Independence Tourism Department, Independence, MO. Website only: visitindependence.com.

Kansas City (KS) Convention and Visitors Bureau. Website only: visitkansascityks.com.

Kansas City Welcome Center, Kansas City, MO (4010 Blue Ridge Cutoff). Open 8 to 5 Monday thru Saturday. ℂ 816-889-3330.

Lawrence Visitor Center, Lawrence, KS (402 N. 2nd St.). Open 8 to 6 May 15 to September 15 and 9 to 5 daily rest of the year. Website: visitlawrence.com. ℂ 785-865-3040. Also see listing on page 155.

Lexington Tourism Bureau, Lexington, MO (927 Main St.). Open 9 to 5 weekdays. Website: visitlexingtonmo.com. ☎ 660-259-4711.

Nevada Tourism Center, Nevada, MO (225 W. Austin Blvd.). Open 9 to 4 Monday thru Saturday, 11 to 3 Sunday. Website: visitnevadamo.com. ☎ 417-667-5300.

Ottawa and Franklin County Visitor Center, Ottawa, KS (2011 E. Logan). Open 8 to 6 daily, May 15 to September 15, 9 to 5 rest of the year. Website: visitottawakansas.com. ☎ 785-242-1411.

St. Joseph Visitor Center, St. Joseph, MO (502 N. Woodbine Rd.). Open 9 to 4 Monday thru Saturday. Website: stjomo.com. ☎ 816-232-1839.

Ideas for Parents and Teachers

The Big Divide and Kids

Looking for something to do this weekend? Consider visiting one of the sites in The Big Divide. *All* of the sites in Chapter 1 are great for kids, as well as the outdoor history sites (page 196). You'll enjoy them too. And don't forget: *Check the websites for special events.* The nature sites are all free with the exception of Remington Nature Center in St. Joseph which charges a small fee.

15 Great Sites for Children

- Arabia Steamboat Museum, Kansas City, MO (page 59)
- Brown v. Board of Education, Topeka, KS (page 211) **FREE**
- Fort Scott National Historic Site, Fort Scott, KS (page 40) **FREE**
- Fort Osage National Historic Landmark, Sibley, MO (page 32)
- George Washington Carver National Monument, Diamond, MO (page 191) **FREE**
- 1859 Jail, Independence, MO (page 148)
- Jesse James Farm and Museum, Kearney, MO (page 175)
- Laura Ingalls Wilder Home, Mansfield, MO (page 188)
- Mahaffie Stagecoach Stop, Olathe, KS (page 57) **FREE** mostly

- Mine Creek Battlefield, Pleasanton, KS (page 171)
- Missouri Town 1855, Lee's Summit, MO (page 80)
- National Frontier Trails Museum, Independence, MO (page 55)
- Old Depot Museum, Ottawa, KS (page 195)
- Patee House Museum, St. Joseph, MO (page 57)
- Pony Express National Museum, St. Joseph, MO (page 63)

10 Ways to Make Your Child's Visit to a Historic Site a Smashing Success

1. Call ahead if you are uncertain about hours, fees, or stroller accessibility. Don't be surprised when you get there!

2. Ask about special events. If you can, schedule your visit around them. Places like Missouri Town 1855 and Mahaffie Stagecoach Stop and Farm are especially fun on these occasions.

3. Find out if they have an orientation film and whether they show it on a schedule or on demand. Plan accordingly. These specialized films (usually 15-20 minutes) are 99 percent worth seeing.

4. Start talking with your child about the upcoming adventure. Have your child help you check the museum or park's website. Check out library books on related topics. The more connections your child has before going, the more he or she will get out of the visit.

5. Locate the historic site on a map. Let your child chart the course — even if you have GPS.

6. Give your child a notebook especially dedicated to travel. Suggest that she use it to record the names of places she visits and to write her own "reviews" of them. If your child likes to draw, have him sketch something at the site.

7. Lend your cell phone or camera to your child. Let her take a few pictures of things that interest her or things she'd like to learn more about. (Ask before using the flash, though.)

8. Give kids as much freedom as possible to explore the site (without bothering others, of course!). For most visitors an hour is plenty of time, but for living history sites you'll probably want to stay longer — maybe even half a day.

9. The gift shop is by the exit for a reason! Decide ahead of time whether to give your kids a small allowance to buy a small souvenir or to say, "We're only browsing today."

10. Keep it light. Keep it fun. Pack a lunch and have a picnic so you can keep talking. Remind children that people in the olden days are not just us with long skirts and funny beards. People who lived 200, 100, or even 50 years ago lived in a different world. They did not know how things would turn out. They thought, for example, that the Civil War would be over in a few months. Are there any things we are doing today that our descendants will say "What were they thinking?" or "How could they have done that?"

Bonus (for budding historians): Ask children to evaluate the site they have just visited. What were the designers of this site trying to convey? How did they choose to convey that message? What exhibits did they choose? Did they succeed? Were they fair? Why or why not?

Reliable Sources for Teaching History to Kids

- **Library of Congress** (loc.gov/index)
  Maps, documents, and photographs.

- **Eyewitness to History** (eyewitnesstohistory.com)
  First-person accounts of historical events with simple explanations.

- **Teaching History** (teachinghistory.org)
  Excellent ideas on how to teach U.S. history.

Resources for Research

Genealogy and Local History

Midwest Genealogy Center

Independence, MO (3440 S. Lee's Summit Rd.). Open 9 to 9 Monday thru Thursday, 9 to 6 Friday, 9 to 5 Saturday, 1 to 5 Sunday. Website: midwestgenealogycenter.org. ℂ 816-252-7228.

One of the nation's premier family history research facilities, with database access and more than 700,000 items including microfilm, maps, periodicals, census and military records, passenger lists, etc.

County museums

These are often treasure troves of information that no one else has collected and preserved — church history, minutes of various clubs, alumni records, tax registries, titles, and small-town newspapers. Call ahead before visiting. These sites usually are staffed by friendly, helpful volunteers. Some will open their doors outside of visiting hours.

Broader Themed Research

Some of the sites in this guide have large research libraries that are open to the public. The most extensive holdings are at the following:

- Harry S. Truman Library (page 205)
- Haskell Indian Nations University (page 215)
- National Frontier Trails Museum (page 55)
- National Military Heritage Museum (page 211)
- National World War I Museum (page 210)
- Pea Ridge National Military Park (page 119)
- Wilson's Creek National Battlefield (page 111)

Other major research centers include:

Black Archives of Mid-America in Kansas City

Kansas City, MO (1722 E. 17th Terrace)

Open 10 to 4 Tuesday thru Thursday, or by appointment. Website: blackarchives.org. For information or to schedule an appointment, call one of the following numbers during business hours: 816-221-1600 or 816-221-1640.

An educational and cultural resource on every aspect of African American life in the Midwest — art, music, sports, medicine, education, civil rights.

Kansas City Public Library — Missouri Valley Room

Kansas City, MO (14 W. 10th St.)

Open 9 to 5 weekdays, 10 to 5 Saturday. Website: kclibrary.org. ✆ 816-701-3427.

A growing, easily accessible collection of Civil War records, maps, periodicals and other items related to Kansas City, Jackson County, and regional history.

Kansas State Historical Society State Archives

Topeka, KS (6425 SW 6th Ave.)

Open 9 to 4:30 Tuesday thru Saturday. Website: kshs.org. ✆ 785-272-8681.

Most comprehensive collection of historical materials in Kansas, including a vast collection of 19th century newspapers.

National Archives

Kansas City, MO (400 W. Pershing)

Research Room open 8 to 4 and exhibits open 9 to 5, Tuesday thru Saturday. Website: archives.gov/kansas-city. ✆ 816-268-8000.

State Historical Society of Missouri (Columbia)

Columbia, MO (1020 Lowry Street)

Open 8 to 4:45 weekdays, 8 to 3:30 Saturday. Website: shs.umsystem.edu. ✆ 816-235-1543.

Works by George Caleb Bingham, Thomas Hart Benton, and other notable Missouri artists are in the State Historical Society's impressive art collection.

State Historical Society of Missouri (Kansas City)

Kansas City, MO (5123 Holmes, 302 Newcomb Hall on the campus of University of Missouri-Kansas City)

Open 8 to 5 weekdays. Website: umkc.edu/whmckc/ ✆ 816-235-1543.

Formerly known as Western Historical Manuscript Collection, site has 13,000 cubic feet of manuscripts.

Book and Film Suggestions
History/Biography

Aron, Stephen. *American Confluence: The Missouri Frontier from Borderland to Border State*. Bloomington: Indiana Univ. Press, 2009.
> How a river valley of fluid political boundaries hardened into the border state of Missouri between 1683 and 1836.

Benedict, Bryce. *Jayhawkers: The Civil War Brigade of James Henry Lane.* Norman: University of Oklahoma Press, 2009.
> Well-researched text tamps down some of the wilder claims about Lane and pins blame for the Osceola raid on James Montgomery.

Brownlee, Richard S. *Gray Ghosts of the Confederacy: Guerrilla Warfare in the West, 1861-1865.* Baton Rouge: LSU Press, 1958.
> A classic text on the guerrilla uprising in Missouri.

Castel, Albert E. and Thomas Goodrich, *Bloody Bill Anderson: The Short, Savage Life of a Civil War Guerrilla.* Mechanicsburg, PA: Stackpole Books, 1998.
> Many observers believe Bloody Bill was the worst of the guerrilla raiders, and after reading this brief, grim book it's hard to argue.

Eickhoff, Diane. *Revolutionary Heart: The Life of Clarina Nichols and the Pioneering Crusade for Women's Rights.* Kansas City: Quindaro Press, 2006.
> A biography of the woman who brought the 19th-century women's rights movement west in the 1850s.

Etcheson, Nicole. *Bleeding Kansas: Contested Liberty in the Civil War Era.* Lawrence: University of Kansas Press, 2004.
> The author argues that most Kansans opposed slavery in their would-be state, not on moral grounds but because they did not want slavery competing with so-called "free labor."

Fellman, Michael. *Inside War: Guerrilla Conflict in Missouri During the American Civil War.* New York: Oxford University Press, 1989.
> Details the Union Army's troublesome role in the conflict between Kansas Jayhawkers and Missouri Bushwhackers.

Foner, Eric: *The Fiery Trial: Abraham Lincoln and American Slavery.* New York: W.W. Norton, 2010.
> Pulitzer Prize-winning book shows how Abraham Lincoln's views on race evolved during his presidency.

Leslie, Edward E. *The Devil Knows How to Ride: The True Story of William Clark Quantrill and His Confederate Raiders.* New York: Da Capo Press, 1998.
> A lively account of Quantrill's life and times.

McCullough, David. *Truman.* New York: Simon & Schuster, 2003.
> Definitive biography of the country's 33rd President.

McPherson, James M. *Battle Cry of Freedom: The Civil War Era.* New York: Oxford University Press, 1988.

> The Civil War, both its political and military history, in one lively, incisive volume — a feat that is hard to beat.

Mutti Burke, Diane. *On Slavery's Border: Missouri's Small-Slaveholding Households, 1815-1865.* Athens: University of Georgia Press, 2010.

> The definitive text on slavery in Missouri details how its slaveholding culture was different from anywhere else.

Neely, Jeremy. *The Border Between Them: Violence and Reconciliation on the Kansas-Missouri Line.* Columbia: University of Missouri Press, 2011.

> Fair-minded look at what happened in six border counties — three in Missouri, three in Kansas — during and after the border wars.

Radiner, Tom. *Caught Between Three Fires: Cass County, Mo., Chaos & Order No. 11 1860-1865.* Xlibris, 2010.

> How the Civil War ripped apart one Missouri county.

Stiles. T.J. *Jesse James: Last Rebel of the Civil War.* New York: Vintage Books, 2003.

> Influential biography explores the historical context for Jesse James and explodes any notion of him as a Robin Hood figure.

White, Christine Schultz. *Now the Wolf Has Gone: The Creek Nation in the Civil War.* College Station: Texas A&M University Press, 1996.

> Account of the events referenced at the Opothle Yahola Memorial (page 117).

Wolk, Gregory. *A Tour Guide to Missouri's Civil War.* Eureka: Monograph Publishing LLC, 2010.

> Mile-by-mile driving guide to what happened where throughout Missouri during the Civil War.

Fiction

Banks, Russell. *Cloudsplitter.* New York: HarperCollins, 1998

> A page-turning pseudo-biography that takes liberties with the facts while trying to penetrate John Brown's fanaticism.

Giles, Paulette. *Enemy Women*. New York: HarperCollins, 2002.

> A searing account of the young women caught in a no-win situation in southwestern Missouri during the Civil War.

Smiley, Jane. *The All-True Travels and Adventures of Lidie Newton*. New York: Ballantine, 1998.

> The story of a free-spirited free-state woman who settles in Kansas during the Border War.

Wilder, Laura Ingalls. *Little House on the Prairie*.

> The classic children's book on pioneering. Typical homesteaders in Kansas, the Ingalls family probably encroached on Osage lands.

Film and TV

August Light (2011)

> The region's premier video company specializing in period reenactments made this film for Wilson's Creek visitor center.

Bad Blood (2007)

> Tells the story of bleeding Kansas with "interviews" of historical subjects and realistic battle simulations.

Lincoln (2012)

> Steven Spielberg's masterful telling of the political drama that led to passage of the Thirteenth Amendment in 1865 begins with a conversation between President Lincoln and two soldiers from the Second Kansas Colored Volunteer Infantry.

The Outlaw Josey Wales (1976)

> Clint Eastwood directed and starred in this movie about a post-Civil War Missourian bent on revenge after the murder of his wife.

Ride with the Devil (1999)

> Ang Lee's film captures the spirit of lawlessness along the Missouri-Kansas border in the Civil War. You may need to watch it more than once to understand all the nuances.

Timeline 1700-1900

U.S. History	Big Divide	The World

Extras

U.S. History

1776 Declaration of Independence

1793 Cotton gin gins up demand for slaves in South

1803 Louisiana Purchase leads to …

1804-06 Lewis and Clark's Corps of Discovery

1812-15 War of 1812

1820 Missouri Compromise

1825 Erie Canal

Big Divide

1700s Osages at peak of power

1700-1850 Fur trade major driver of region's economy

1811 George Caleb Bingham born

1821 Missouri statehood

1821 Santa Fe Trail

1827 Fort Leavenworth

1760–1820 First Industrial Revolution

The World

1776 Adam Smith's *The Wealth of Nations*

1789 French Revolution begins; leads to rise of Napoleon (below)

1804 Haiti independence

1810 Mexico independence

1813 *Pride and Prejudice* (Jane Austen, below)

1815 Napoleon's Waterloo

1820 Antarctica discovered

1822 Brazilian independence

U.S. History	Big Divide	The World
1830 Indian Removal Act creates tribal reserves (see map, page 28)	**1830** Oregon Trail	
		**1833** Britain ends slavery
1836 Texans defeated at Alamo		**1837** Queen Victoria's reign begins
1839 Bicycle invented	**1830** Shawnee Indian Mission	**1839** First Opium War
	1836 Platte Purchase expands Missouri	**1842** Anesthesia
	**1838** Mormon War and expulsion; Joseph Smith (below) and other leaders jailed	
1844 Morse telegraph		
1846–48 Mexican War		
1850 Fugitive Slave Act		
1850 First national women's rights convention		**1845–49** Irish potato famine; families flee to U.S.
1853 *Uncle Tom's Cabin*	**1853** Fort Riley	**1853** Perry in Japan
1854 Kansas-Nebraska Act	**1854** Kansas Territory opens	**1853–56** Crimean War creates huge demand for U.S. exports, especially Northern grain and Southern cotton
1854 *Walden*	**1856** Pottawatomie massacre	
	1856 Battle of Black Jack	
1857 Dred Scott Supreme Court decision	**1858** Lecompton Constitution defeated	

(see map, page 28)

Extras

U.S. History	Big Divide	The World

U.S. History

1859 Harpers Ferry raid; John Brown hanged

1861 Eleven states secede to form Confederacy

1862 Congress passes Homestead Act, Morrill Act (land grants), and Pacific Railroad Act

1863 President Lincoln issues Emancipation Proclamation

1865 13th Amendment ends slavery

1865 Lincoln assassinated

Big Divide

PONY EXPRESS
APR 3
SAN FRANCISCO

1860-61 Pony Express service

1860-70 Tribal nations removed to Oklahoma

1861 Kansas statehood

1861 Battle of Wilson's Creek

1862 Battle of Pea Ridge

1863 Quantrill's Raid and Gen'l Order No. 11

1864 Price's Raid leads to Battle of Westport and Battle of Mine Creek

1864 George Washington Carver born

1861–65 American Civil War

The World

1859 Darwin's *Origin of the Species*

1861 Serf emancipation in Russia

1863 First subway (London)

1865 *Alice in Wonderland*

U.S. History	Big Divide	The World

U.S. History

1866 Ku Klux Klan formed to oppose Reconstruction

1869 Trans-continental R.R.

1870 Black male suffrage (15th Amendment)

1872 First national park (Yellowstone)

1876 Custer's army routed at Little Big Horn

1876 Telephone

1881 Clara Barton forms American Red Cross

1896 *Plessy v. Ferguson* keeps schools segregated until *Brown v. Board*

Big Divide

1866 Buffalo Soldiers organized

1867 Chisholm Trail opened

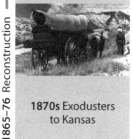

1870s Exodusters to Kansas

1873 Barbed wire

1884 Jesse James killed; Harry Truman born

The World

1866 Alfred Nobel invents dynamite

1867 Suez Canal

1867 Canada established

1869 *War and Peace*

1870 Lister's antiseptic methods advance

1876 Great Chinese famine

1879 Albert Einstein born

1881 First electrical power plant (Britain)

1883 *Treasure Island*

1884 Oxford English Dictionary

1889 Aspirin

1865–76 Reconstruction

1876-1914 "The Gilded Age"

1871-1914 Second Industrial Revolution

Extras

Index

A

Adair, Rev. Samuel and Florella 89
Alexander Majors House (Kansas City, MO) 52, 62–63, 129
Amelia Earhart Birthplace Museum (Atchison, KS) 129, 204, 218
Amelia Earhart Earthworks (Atchison, KS) 219
Amelia Earhart Festival 219
American Jazz Museum. *See* Negro Leagues Baseball Museum
Americans by Choice (exhibit) 221–222
Anderson, "Bloody Bill" 99, 139, 148, 164, 165
Anita B. Gorman Discovery Center (Kansas City, MO) 18
Anthony, Daniel 73
Arabia Steamboat Museum (Kansas City, MO) 51, 59–60, 125
Armstrong, Louis 214
Arrow Rock, Missouri (Historic Arrow Rock) 126, 128, 152
Atchison, David Rice 72
Atchison, Kansas
　Amelia Earhart Birthplace Museum 129, 204, 218
　Amelia Earhart Earthworks 219
　Atchison County Historical Society Museum and Visitor Center 203, 217
　Atchison Visitor Center 223
　Outdoor Rail Museum 217
Atchison, Topeka and Santa Fe Railroad 78, 203, 217

B

Baker Creek (Mansfield, MO) 189
Baldwin City, Kansas
　Black Jack Battlefield and Nature Park 91–92, 127
Basie, Count 203

Bass, Phyllis 184–185
Bates County, Missouri 140, 146
Bates County Museum (Butler, MO) 126, 131, 160
Battle of Carthage State Historic Site (Carthage, MO) 111, 127
Battle of Island Mound State Historic Site (near Butler, MO) 126, 127, 131, 138, 146
Battle of Lexington State Historic Site (Lexington, MO) 105, 113–114, 127, 129
Battle of the Hemp Bales. *See* Battle of Lexington
Battle of Westport Battleground and Museum (Kansas City, MO) 127, 166, 169–170
Battles. *See also* individual place names
Baxter Springs, Kansas
　Baxter Springs Heritage Center and Museum 141, 158, 158–160
　Baxter Springs Route 66 Visitor Center 223
　Soldiers' Lot 160, 167
Beach Museum of Art (Manhattan, KS) 86, 128
Beecher Bible and Rifle Church (near Wamego, KS) 8, 12
Beecher, Henry Ward 10–11
Benton, Rita 206
Benton, Thomas Hart 45, 84, 128, 152, 159, 201, 205, 206–207
Bingham, George Caleb 45, 58, 128, 139, 141, 150–153, 173, 232
Bingham-Waggoner Estate (Independence, MO) 128, 129, 152–153
Black Jack Battlefield and Nature Park (near Baldwin City, KS) 76, 91–92, 127
Bleeding Kansas 29, 57, 79, 80, 91
Blodgett, Wells 109
Blue Room and Gem Theater (Kansas City, MO) 202, 214

About the Authors

Diane Eickhoff, an editor turned historian, published her first biography, *Revolutionary Heart,* with Quindaro Press in 2006. It was named a Kansas Notable Book by the State Library of Kansas and honored with a Willa Cather Award and *ForeWord's* gold medal for biography. She lectures regularly for the Kansas Humanities Council on the women's rights movement before, during, and after the Civil War.

Aaron Barnhart was television critic for the *Kansas City Star* from 1997 to 2012. He has contributed to *The New York Times, Village Voice, Entertainment Weekly,* MSNBC's *Hardball,* CNN's *Reliable Sources,* APM's *Marketplace,* and *Macworld.* His 2010 collection of columns was *Tasteland,* also from Quindaro.

They are married and live in Kansas City, Missouri — two blocks east of the Missouri-Kansas state line. They have four grandchildren, to whom *The Big Divide* is dedicated.

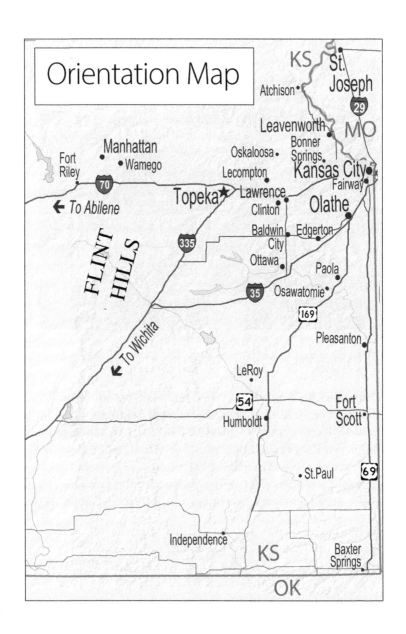

Orientation Map

KS
Atchison
St. Joseph
🛡29
Leavenworth MO
Manhattan
Oskaloosa Bonner Springs
Fort Riley Wamego
Lecompton Kansas City
🛡70 Fairway
← To Abilene Topeka ★ Lawrence
Clinton Olathe
FLINT HILLS Baldwin City Edgerton
🛡335 Ottawa
🛡35 Paola
Osawatomie
🛡169
Pleasanton
← To Wichita
LeRoy
🛡54 Fort Scott
Humboldt
St. Paul 🛡69
Independence
KS Baxter Springs
OK